RUSSIAN
ARMORED
FIGHTING VEHICLES

GEORGE BRADFORD

STACKPOLE
BOOKS

Published by
STACKPOLE BOOKS
5067 Ritter Road
Mechanicsburg, PA 17055
www.stackpolebooks.com

Cover design by Wendy A. Reynolds

Printed in the United States of America

10 9 8 7 6 5 4 3 2 1

FIRST EDITION

Library of Congress Cataloging-in-Publication Data

Bradford, George.
  Russian armored fighting vehicles / George Bradford. — 1st ed.
      p. cm. — (World War II AFV plans)
  Includes bibliographical references.
  ISBN-13: 978-0-8117-3356-4
  ISBN-10: 0-8117-3356-4
  1. Armored vehicles, Military—Soviet Union—Drawings. 2. Tanks
(Military science)—Soviet Union—Drawings. I. Title.

  UG446.5.B26826 2007
  623.7'4750947—dc22
                                                          2006101099

Contents

Introduction

This third volume in this series of books on scale drawings of armored fighting vehicles of World War II is devoted to Russian military vehicles which appeared just before and during World War II. Many of these vehicles were either in use or in development well before war broke out, and are shown here roughly in chronological order of appearance on the scene. However, there was much overlap in vehicle production, and this makes it somewhat difficult to establish a sequence which is totally perfect.

Therefore, if you are looking for armored vehicles that used by Russian forces before and during World War II, then you should be able to find most of them in this book. Among the vehicles covered you will find some of the prototypes that never really saw action, plus some of the vehicles that were just too late to participate in the war. You will also find that we cover mainly armored fighting vehicles, but also with a few support vehicles that fought along side of them thrown in.

The ultimate purpose of this series of books is to try and present a sequence of World War II military vehicle plan view scale drawings all in one place. Most of these drawings display 4-view plans, but with some of the smaller vehicles we were able to show five or more views. However, no matter how well the plans are drawn it is always necessary to have sufficient photo reference books as well. There are a number of "walk around" and close up view series on the market to give the super detailers all the finer detail they could ask for.

Over the years, scale drawings of various armored vehicles have appeared in magazines and books, but never all in one place where they would be easy for the researcher or modeler to access them. Many different scales have fought for the limelight, but the more popular ones of late have boiled down to mainly 1:35, 1:48 and 1:72 in the armor modeling world. With this in mind we have tried to keep the drawings as large as possible with a preponderance of 1:35 scale drawings, supported by 1:48 scale where appropriate, and also for vehicles that are simply too big to fit on these pages comfortably as 1:35 scale drawings. The 1:72 scale plans are mainly used to fill out a page here and there, and give the modeler some choice.

You will also find a chart at the beginning of this book for reducing or enlarging any of these drawings to other popular scales. The quality and accuracy of modern photocopying should make it possible for you to achieve whatever final scale you require. However, in some cases where enlargement is required, you may only be able to squeeze one view onto letter size paper and may have to utilize 11" x 17" paper where available.

These drawings have been created using vector based drawing applications with line weights ranging from .25 point to 1 point, and thus should easily hold the finer detail when copying. The bulk of these drawings were done over a period of ten years and are currently among the most precise and accurate AFV drawings available. You will also notice a variance in the drawings as the art style changes slightly over the years, but eventually supports shading in the majority of the later works.

SCALE
CONVERSIONS

REDUCING

1:35 to 1:48 Scale = 73%

1:35 to 1:76 Scale = 46%

1:35 to 1:72 Scale = 49%

1:35 to 1:87 Scale = 41%

1:48 to 1:76 Scale = 63%

1:48 to 1:72 Scale = 66%

1:48 to 1:87 Scale = 55%

1:72 to 1:76 Scale = 95%

ENLARGING

1:35 to 1:32 Scale = 109%

1:35 to 1:16 Scale = 218%

1:48 to 1:35 Scale = 138%

1:48 to 1:32 Scale = 150%

1:48 to 1:16 Scale = 300%

1:72 to 1:35 Scale = 207%

1:72 to 1:48 Scale = 150%

1:72 to 1:16 Scale = 450%

BA-27 (1928)

on the AMO-F-15 truck chassis
and later on the Ford AA chassis

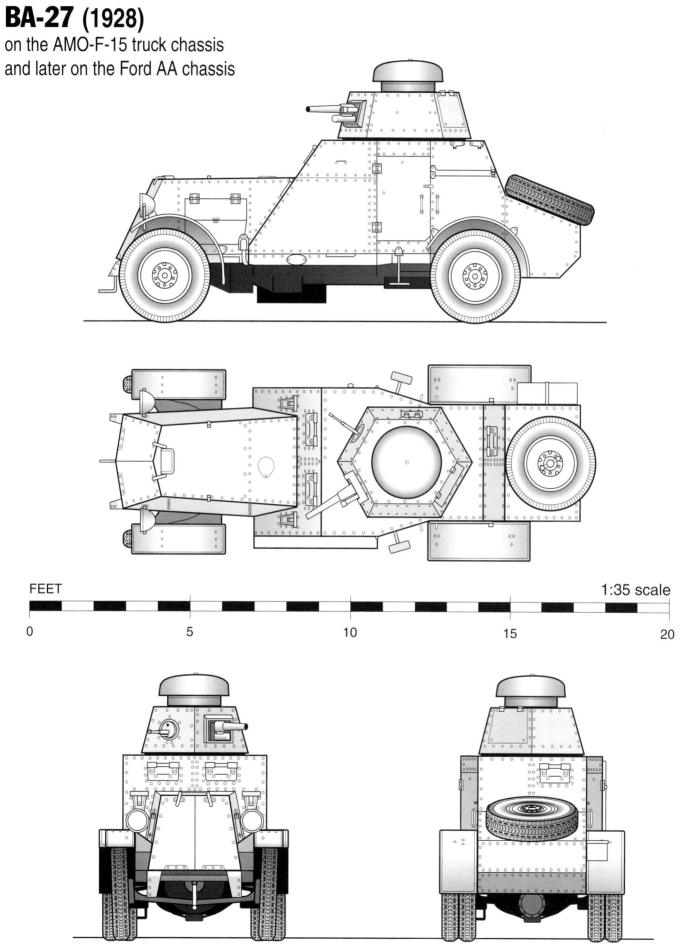

FEET

1:35 scale

0   5   10   15   20

FAI-M Armored Car (1938)
on the GAZ-M-1 chassis

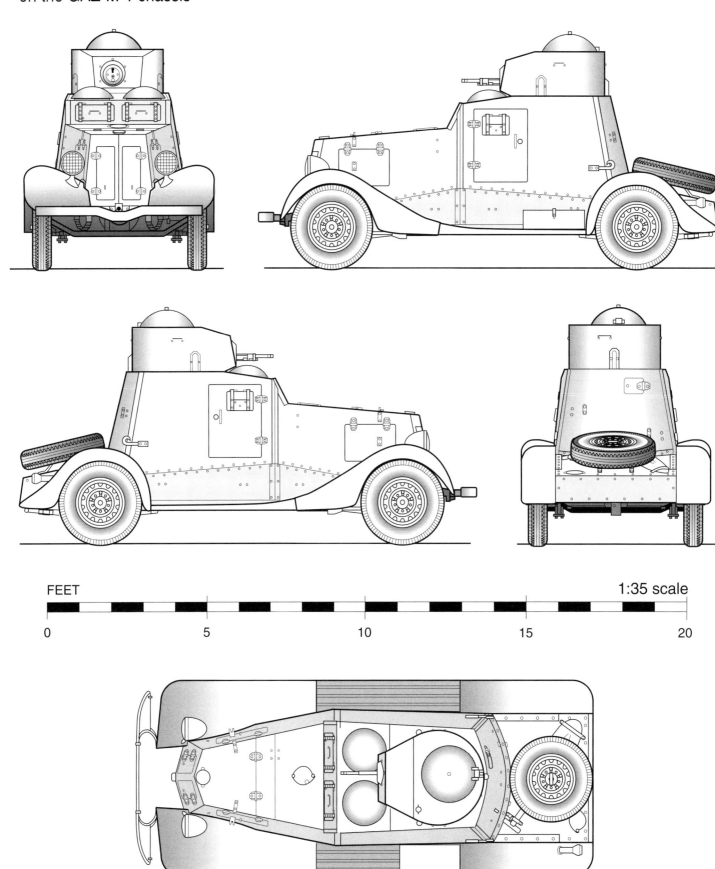

FEET

1:35 scale

0 5 10 15 20

BA-27M (1931)
on the Ford-Timken chassis

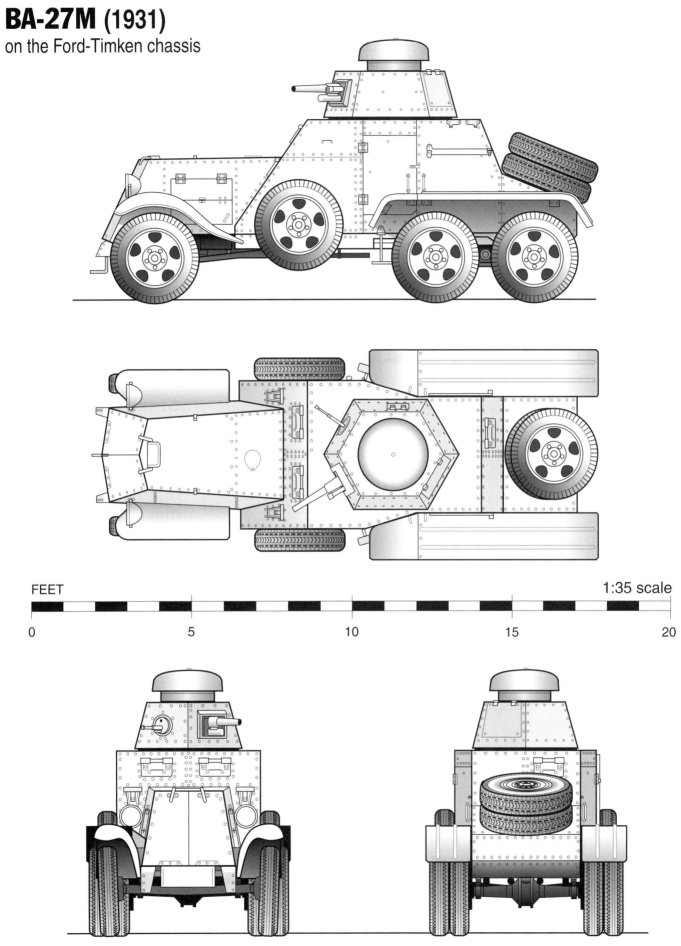

FEET

1:35 scale

0   5   10   15   20

T-26 Model 1931 Light Tank
(with T-26TU command tank aerial and 37mm gun turret shown)

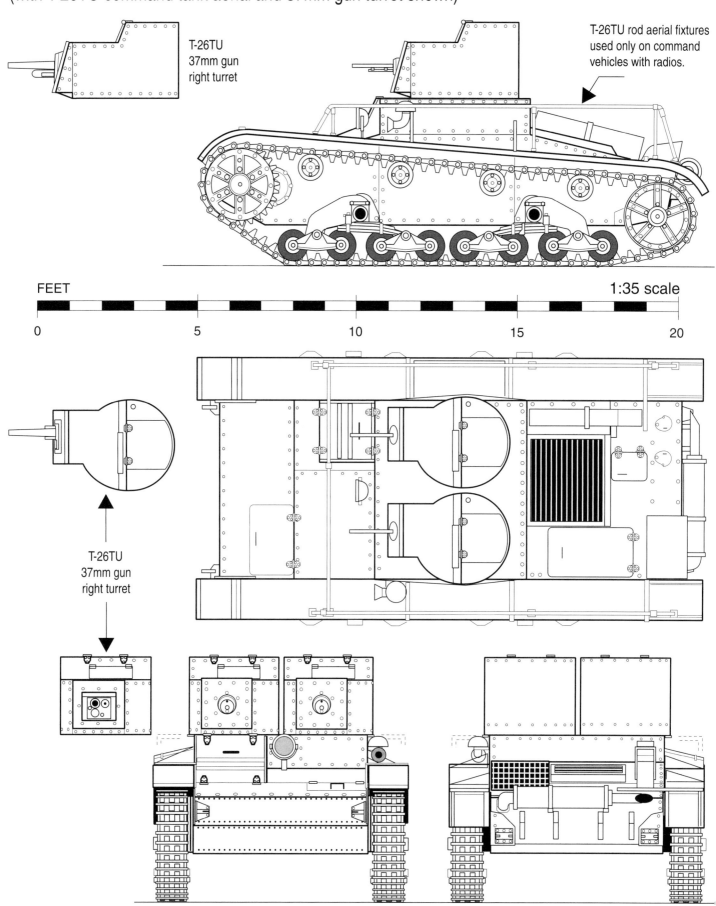

T-26TU
37mm gun
right turret

T-26TU rod aerial fixtures
used only on command
vehicles with radios.

FEET

1:35 scale

0   5   10   15   20

T-26TU
37mm gun
right turret

T-24 Medium (1932)

FEET   1:35 scale

0   5   10

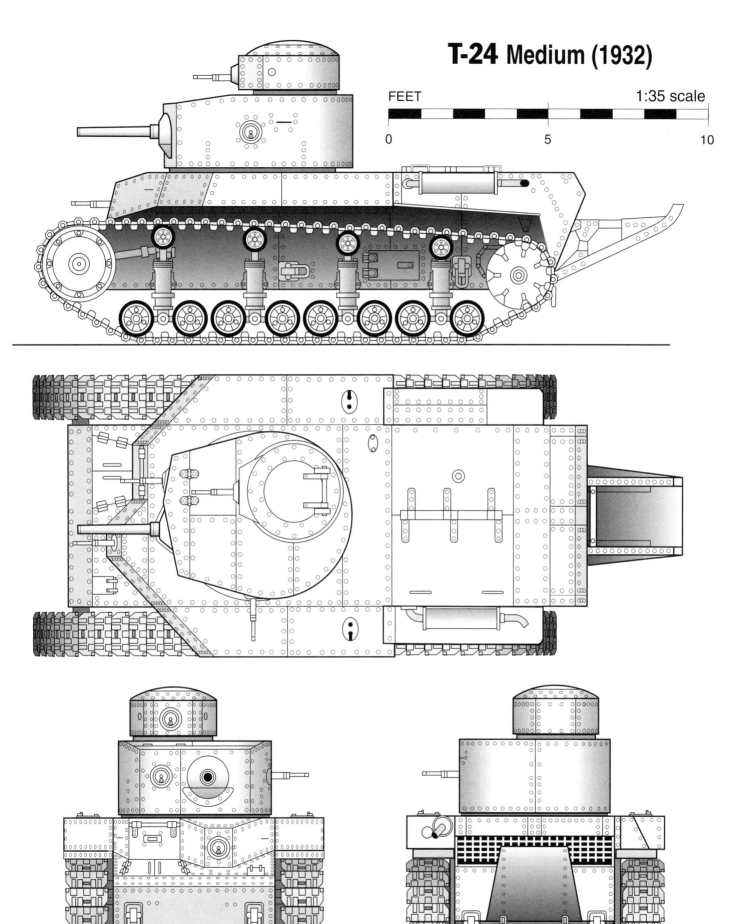

BT-2 (Bystrochodnyj Tank)
Model 1932 Fast Tank, early production

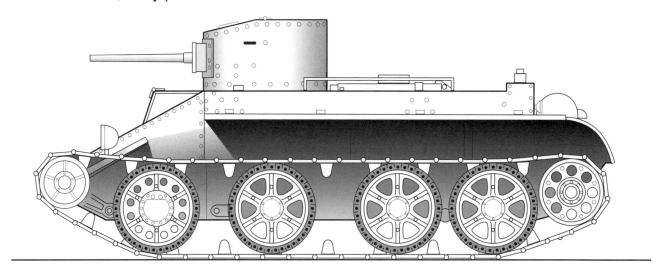

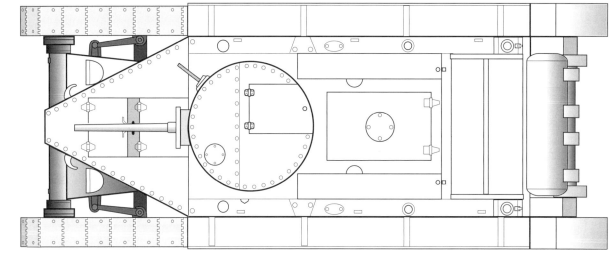

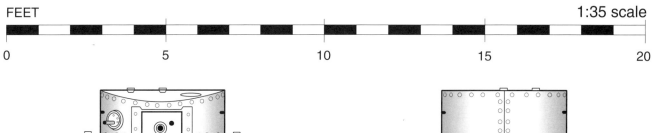

FEET

1:35 scale

0   5   10   15   20

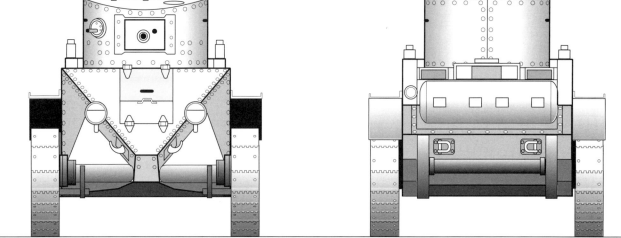

A Russian BT-5 knocked out in the early German advances.

A group of BT tanks overtaken during the German advance.

BT-5 (Bystrochodnyj Tank)
Model 1934 Fast Tank, standard production turret

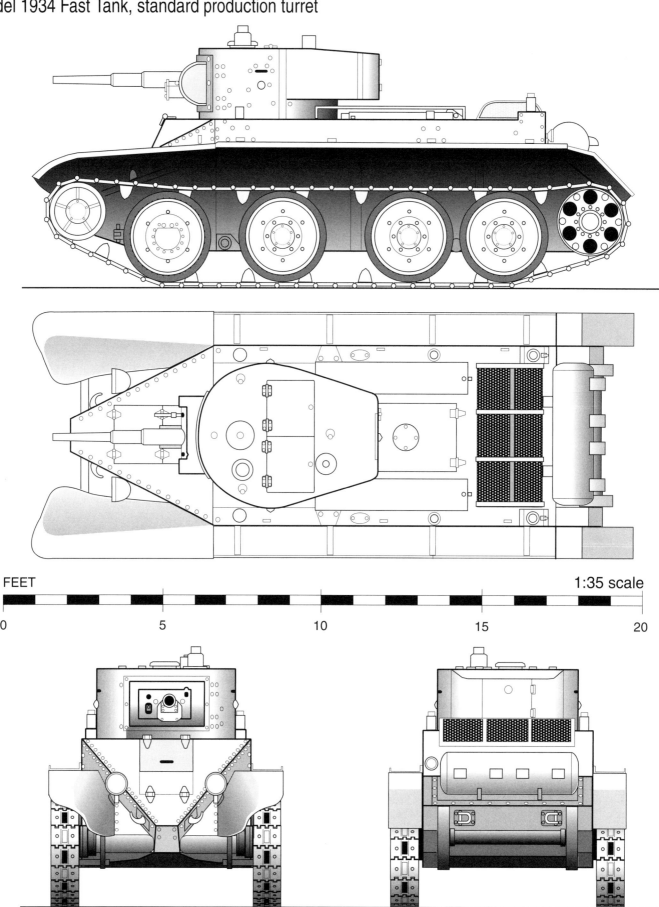

FEET

1:35 scale

0   5   10   15   20

OT-26 Flamethrower Tank

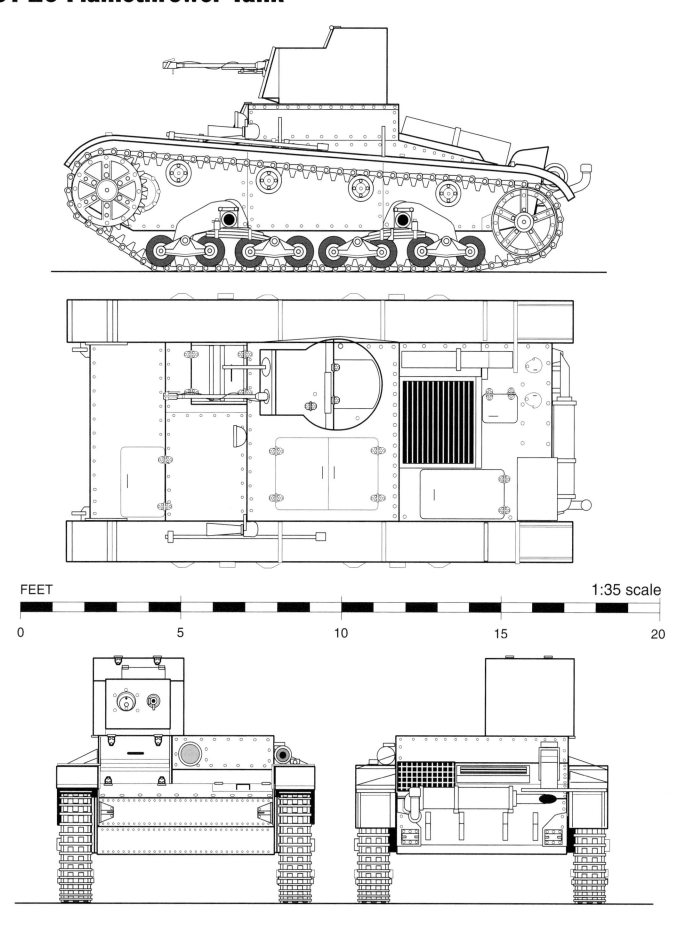

FEET   1:35 scale

0   5   10   15   20

A BA-10 heavy armored car being inspected by German troops.

A pair of T-26 tanks during the Winter War with Finland.

BA-10M Model 1939
Medium Armored Car

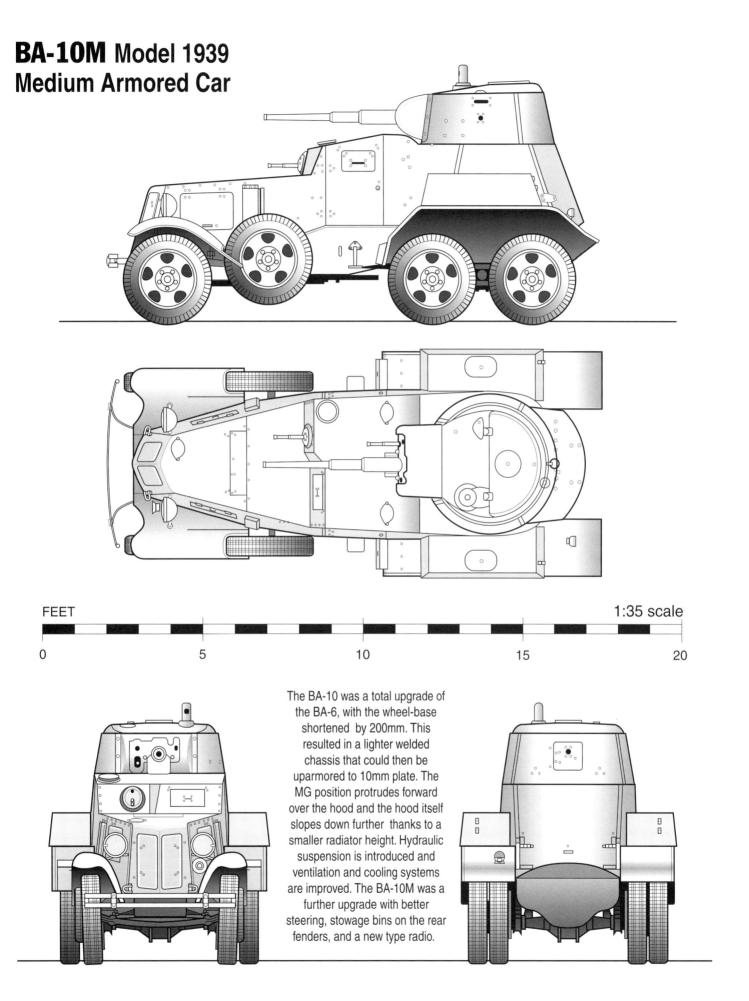

FEET

1:35 scale

0   5   10   15   20

The BA-10 was a total upgrade of the BA-6, with the wheel-base shortened by 200mm. This resulted in a lighter welded chassis that could then be uparmored to 10mm plate. The MG position protrudes forward over the hood and the hood itself slopes down further thanks to a smaller radiator height. Hydraulic suspension is introduced and ventilation and cooling systems are improved. The BA-10M was a further upgrade with better steering, stowage bins on the rear fenders, and a new type radio.

T-28 Model 1934

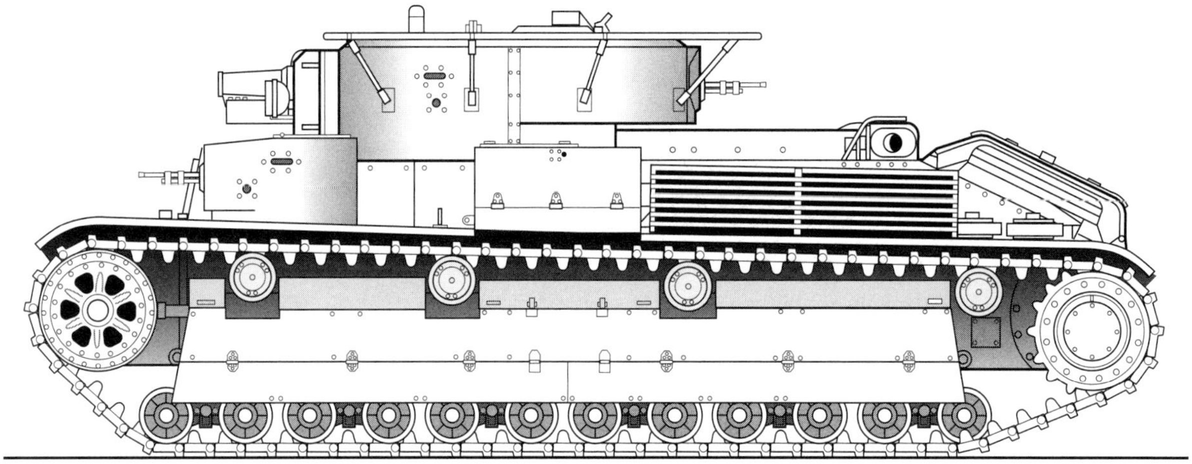

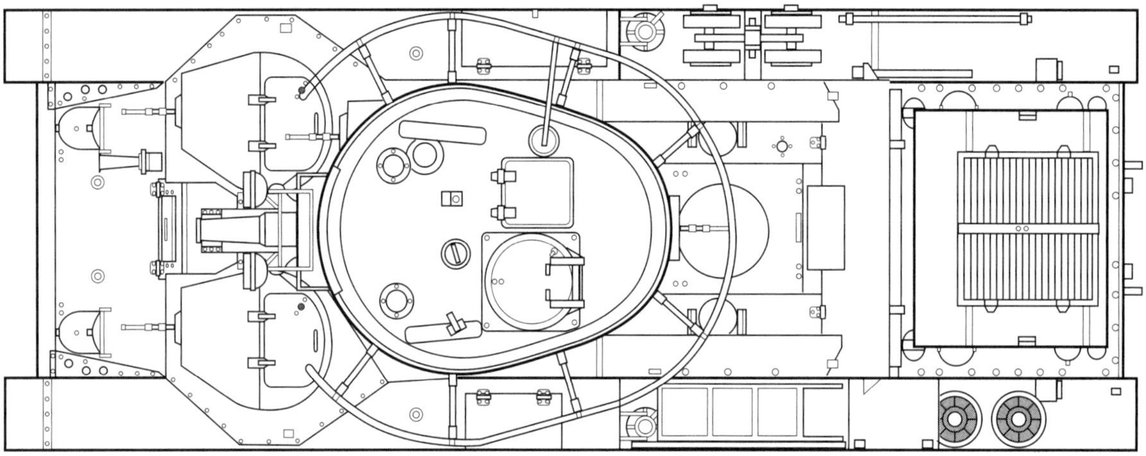

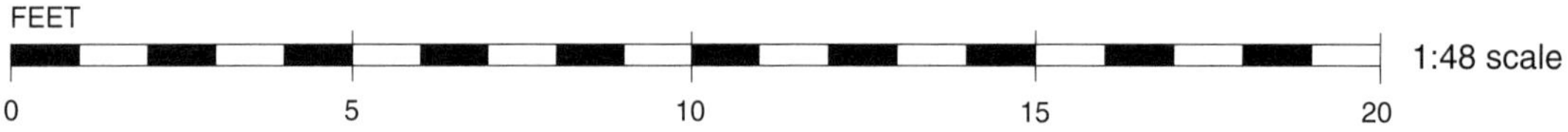
FEET
0
5
10
15
20
1:48 scale

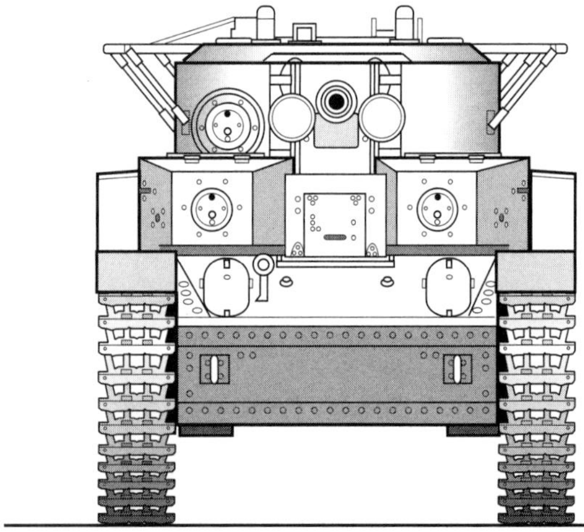

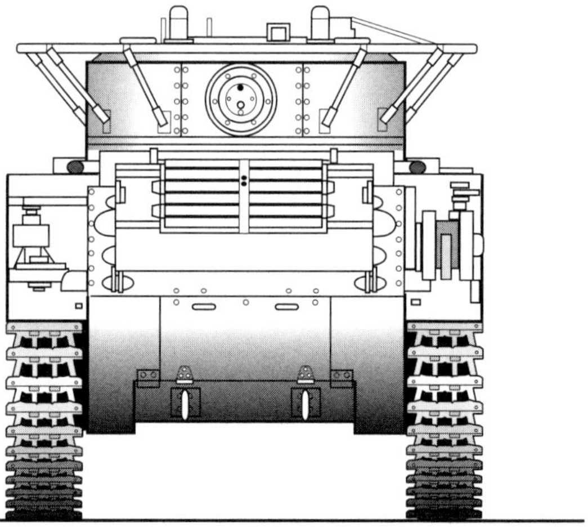

T-35 Model 1935

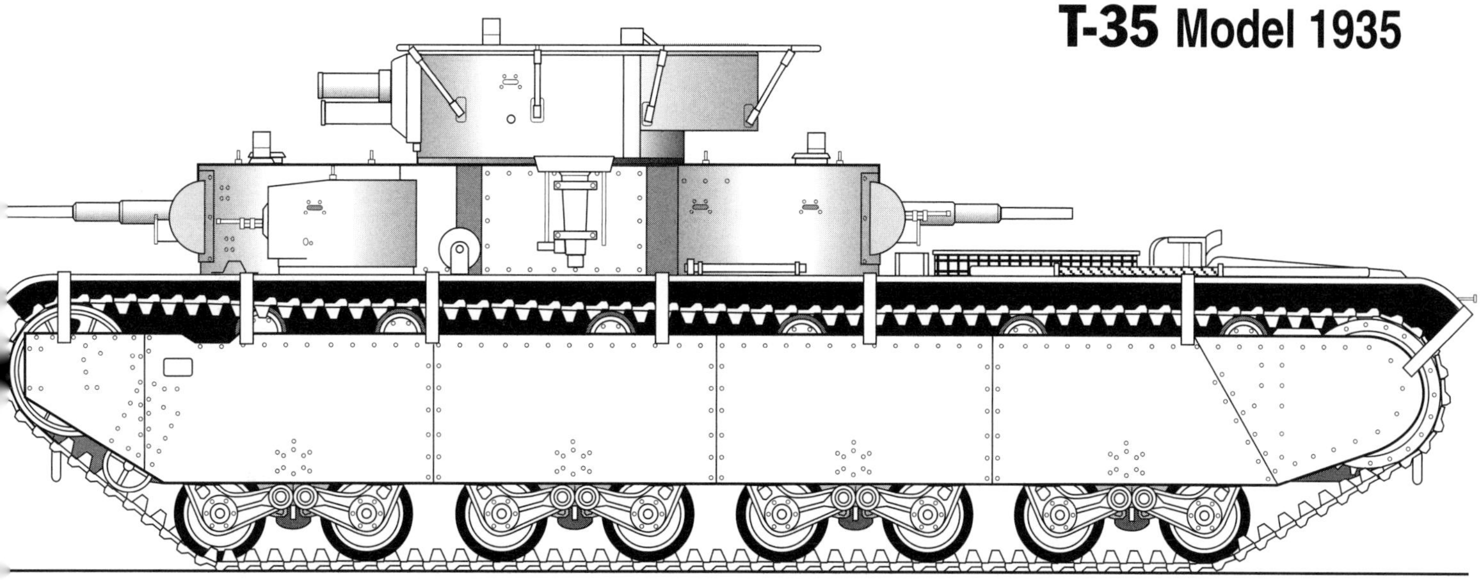

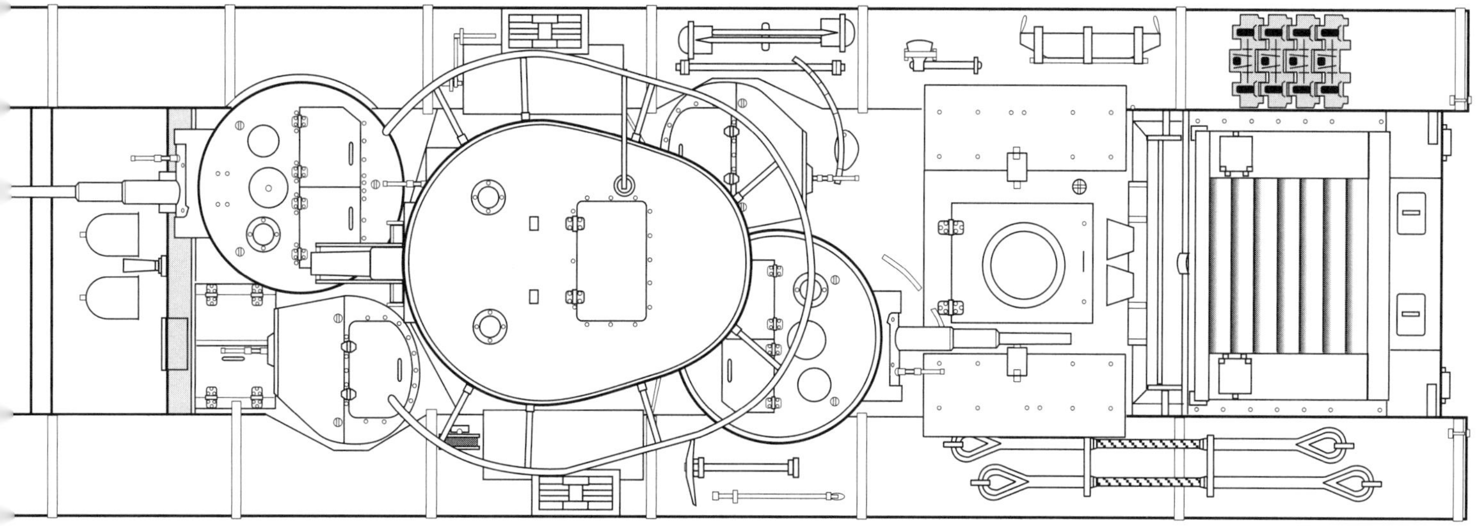

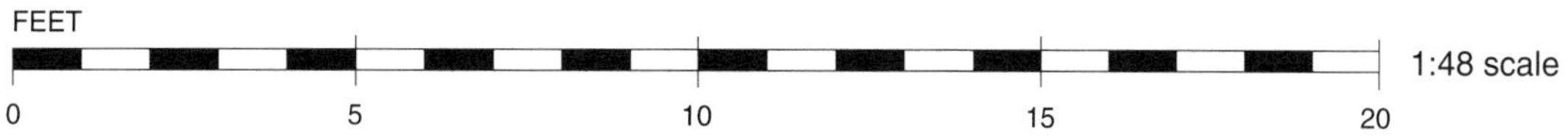
FEET
0
5
10
15
20
1:48 scale

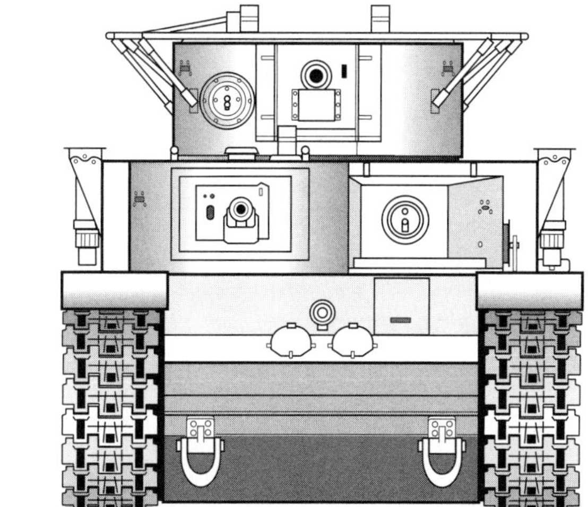

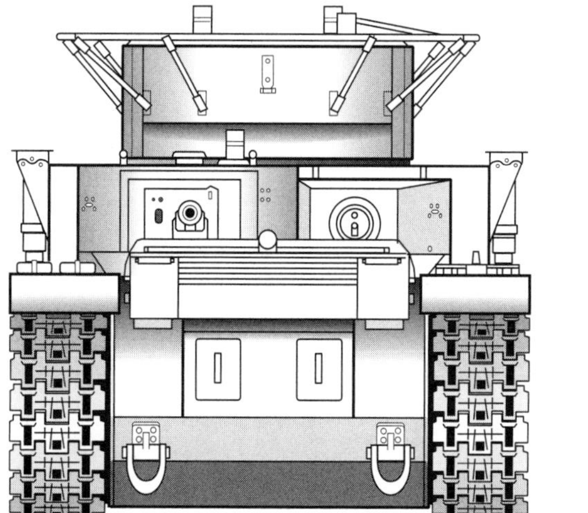

The Russian multi-turreted T-35 was an unwieldy heavy tank at best, and proved to be nearly useless during blitzkrieg attacks.

T-28 Model 1934

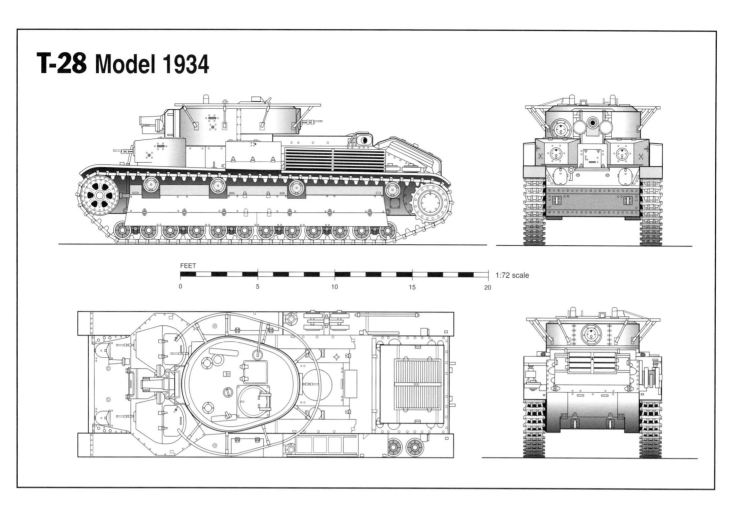

FEET

0   5   10   15   20   1:72 scale

T-35 Model 1935

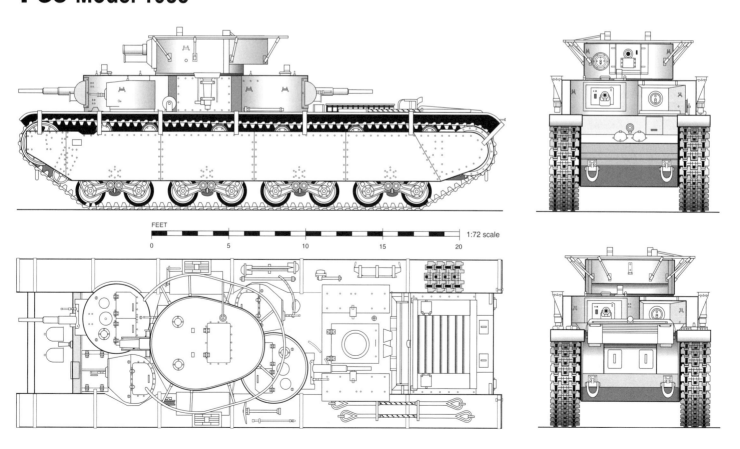

FEET

0   5   10   15   20   1:72 scale

T-26 Model 1933 Light Tank

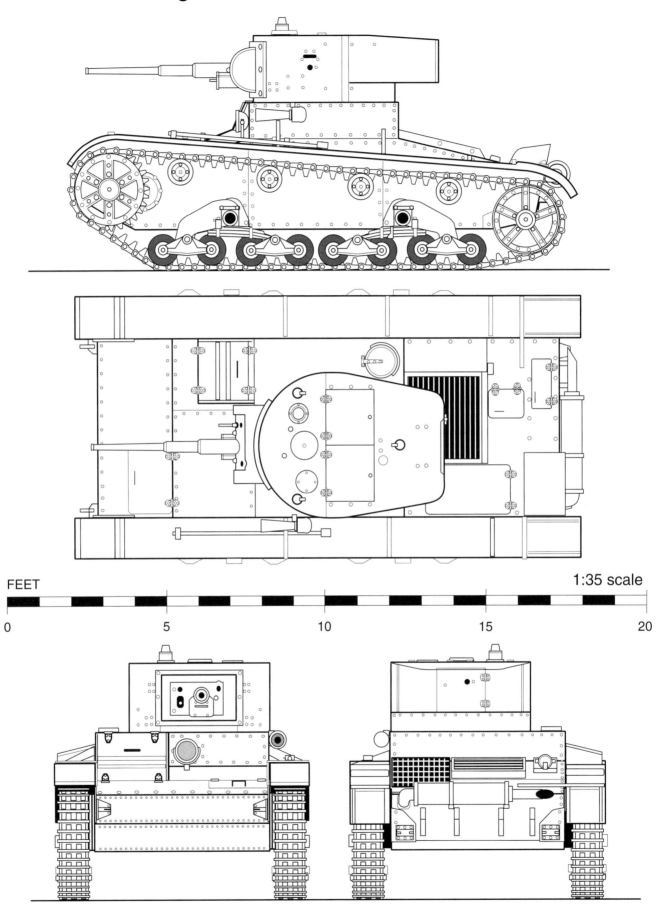

FEET

1:35 scale

0   5   10   15   20

T-26TU Model 1933 Command Tank
(with drop forged mantlet)

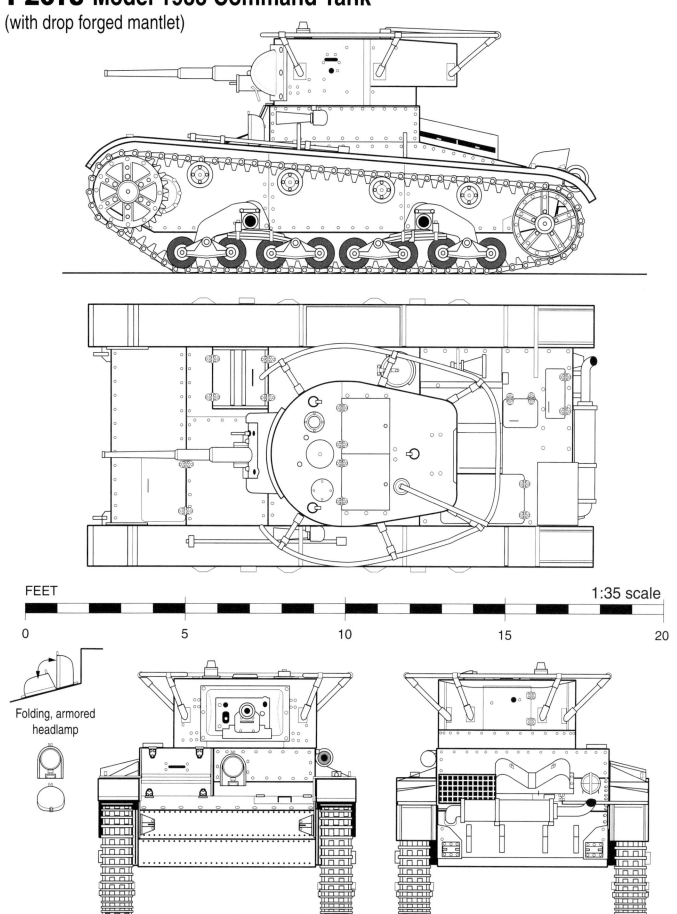

FEET

1:35 scale

0   5   10   15   20

Folding, armored
headlamp

Russian T-26 tanks supplied to the Chinese in Yunan province, 1940.

A good view of the rear deck of a T-26.

BA-20V Command Version (1936)

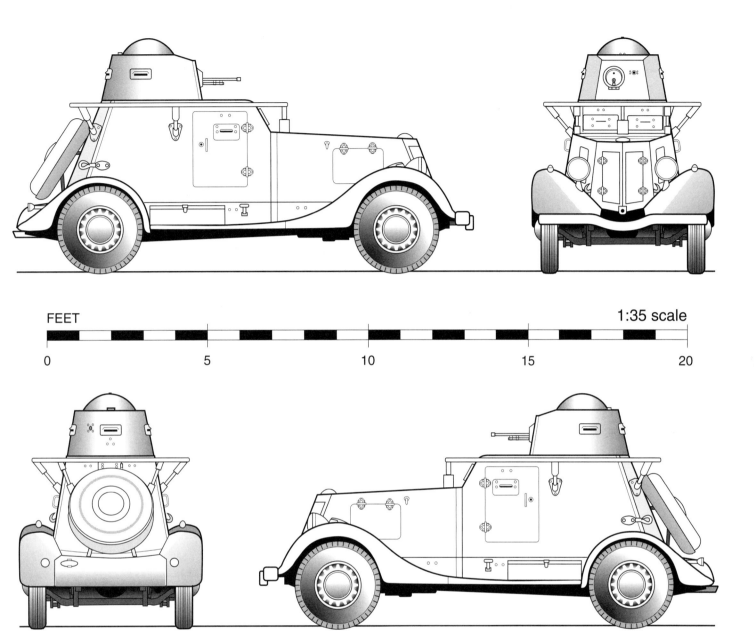

FEET   1:35 scale

0   5   10   15   20

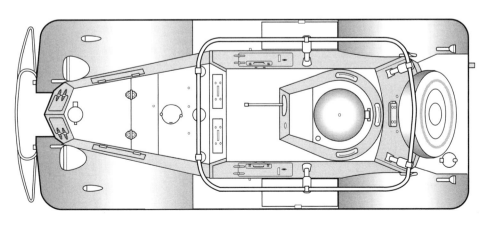

A series of light armored cars meant to be scout vehicles were developed in the early 1930s. The FAI, with its vertical turret sides, was based on the GAZ-M1 Ford chassis, and led up to the BA-20. The early BA-20V command version carried a frame aerial as shown here. The later BA-20M command version did away with the frame aerial, and carried a whip aerial first on the front hood and eventually on the left side of the hull.

With a crew of two and a top speed of 47 mph, it had a range of 280 miles.

T-26
Model 1933 Light Tank
(with final production turret)

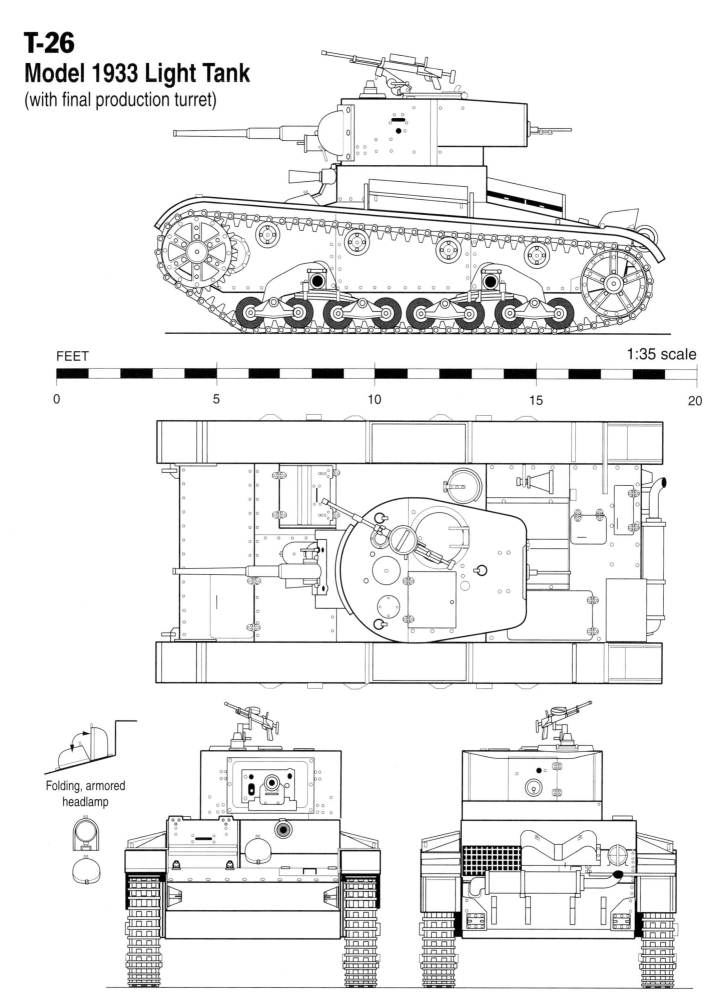

FEET

1:35 scale

0   5   10   15   20

Folding, armored
headlamp

T-26A Artillery Support Tank

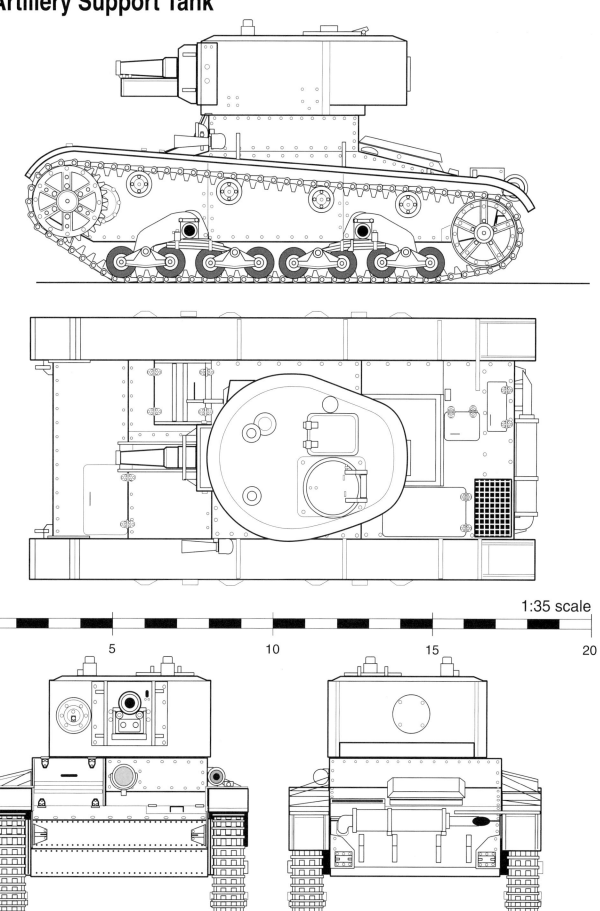

FEET   1:35 scale

0   5   10   15   20

OT-130
Flamethrower Tank
(late version)

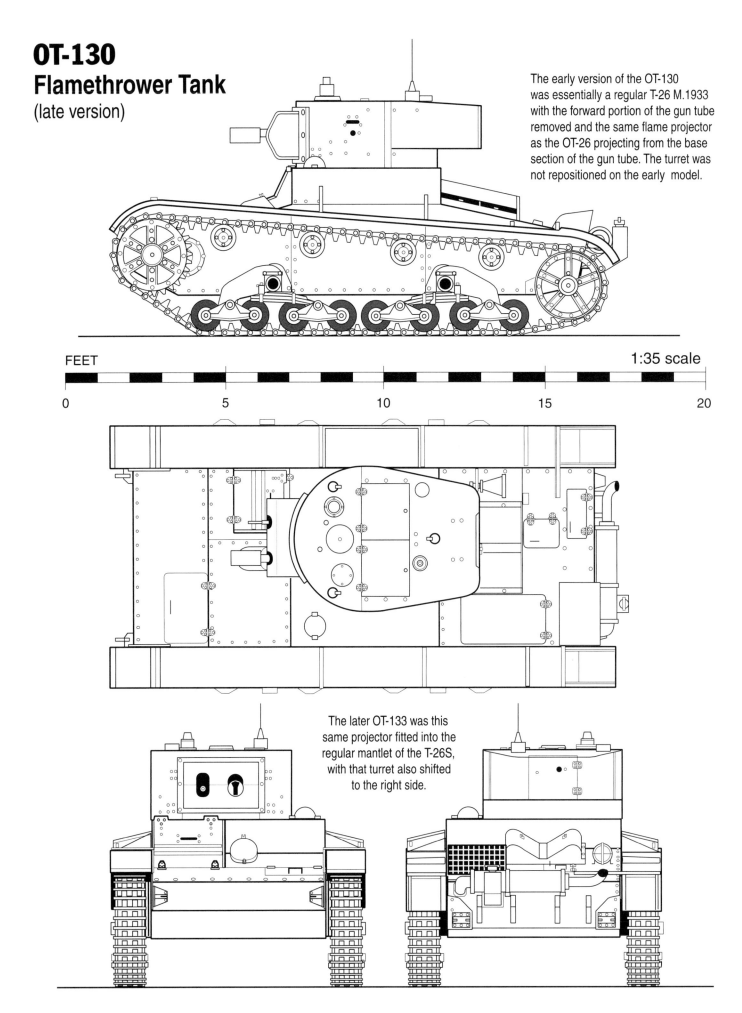

The early version of the OT-130 was essentially a regular T-26 M.1933 with the forward portion of the gun tube removed and the same flame projector as the OT-26 projecting from the base section of the gun tube. The turret was not repositioned on the early model.

FEET

1:35 scale

0   5   10   15   20

The later OT-133 was this same projector fitted into the regular mantlet of the T-26S, with that turret also shifted to the right side.

T-38 Model 1937
Light Amphibious Tank

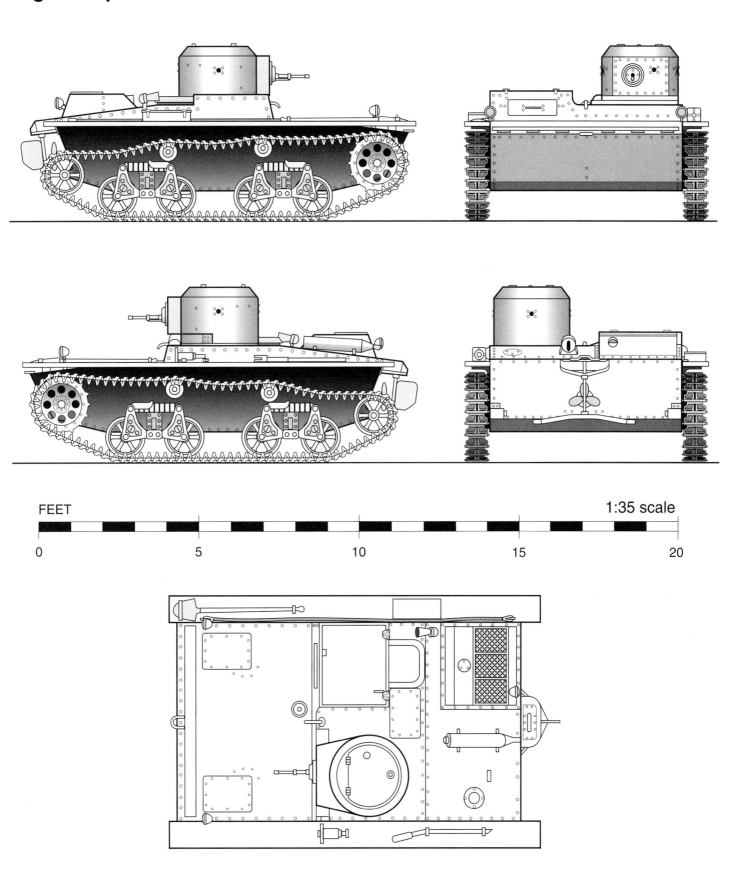

FEET

1:35 scale

0   5   10   15   20

A pair of T-38 Amphibious Light Tanks on maneuvers in Russia, 1939.

T-26S Model 1937 Light Tank

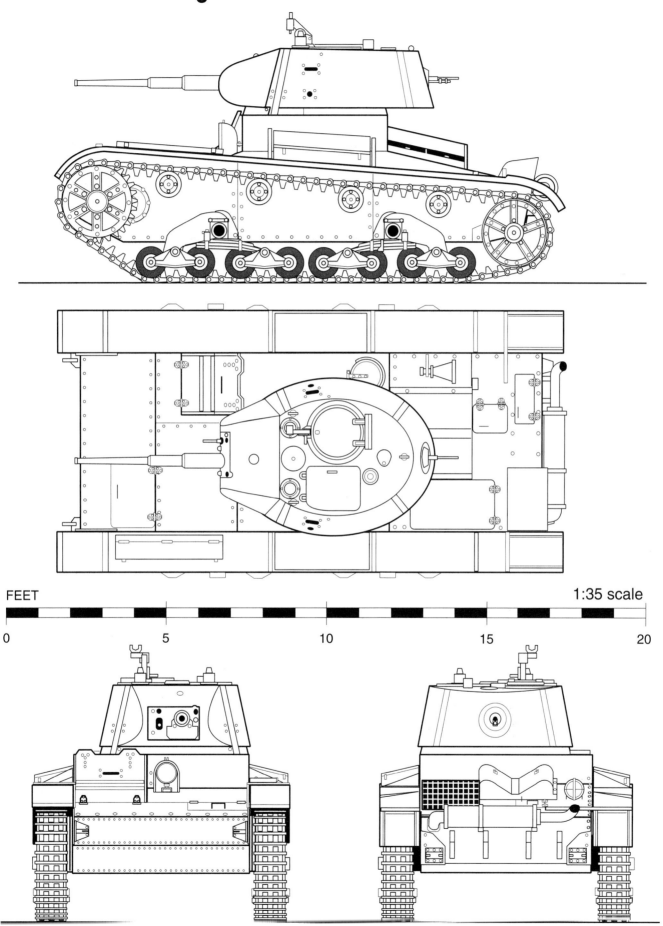

FEET

1:35 scale

0   5   10   15   20

T-26S Model 1939 Light Tank

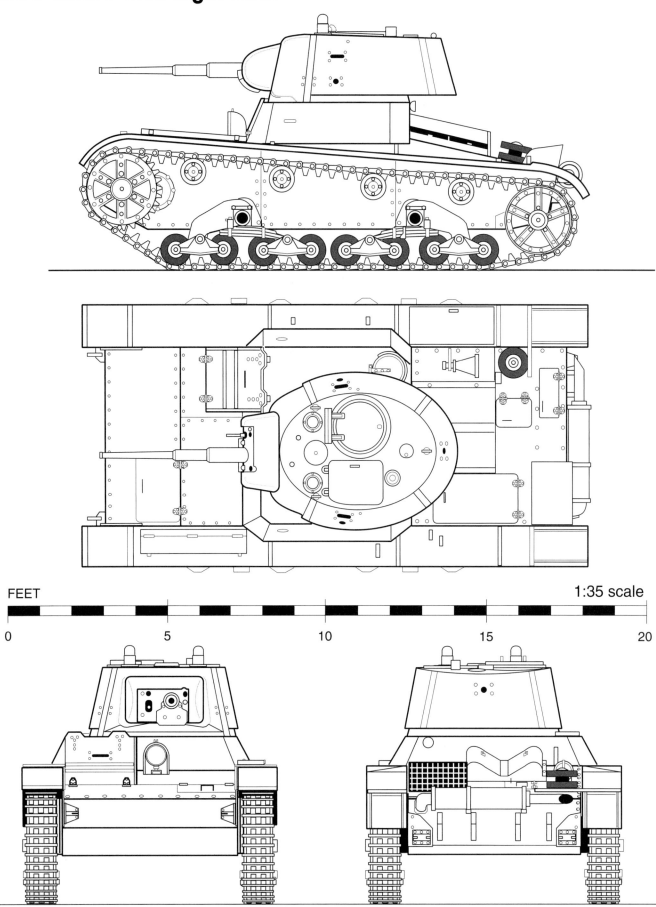

FEET

1:35 scale

0   5   10   15   20

BA-64B
Model 1943 Light Armored Car

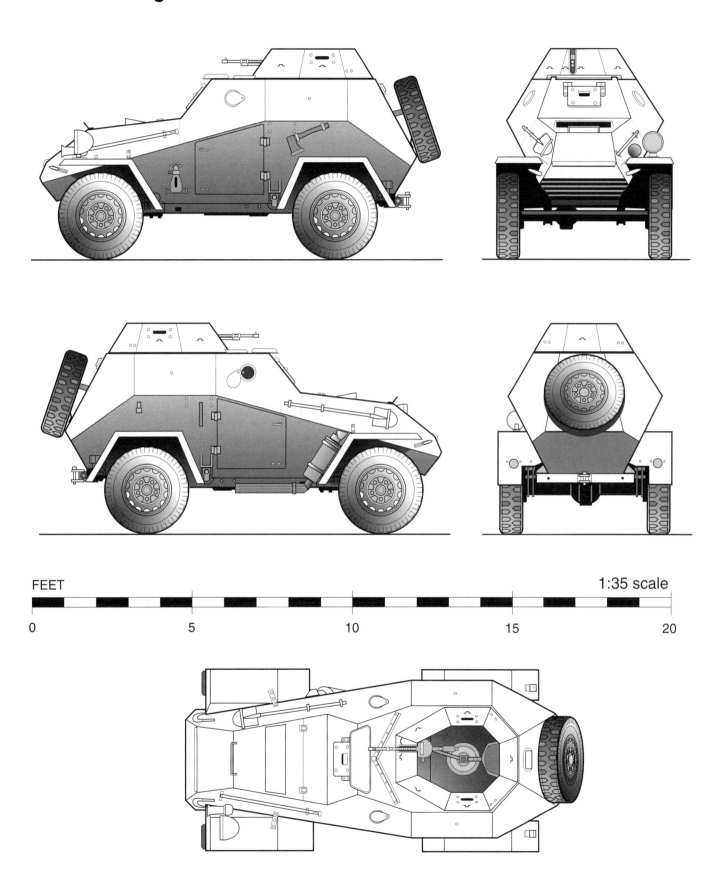

FEET

1:35 scale

0   5   10   15   20

BT-7 (Model 1937)

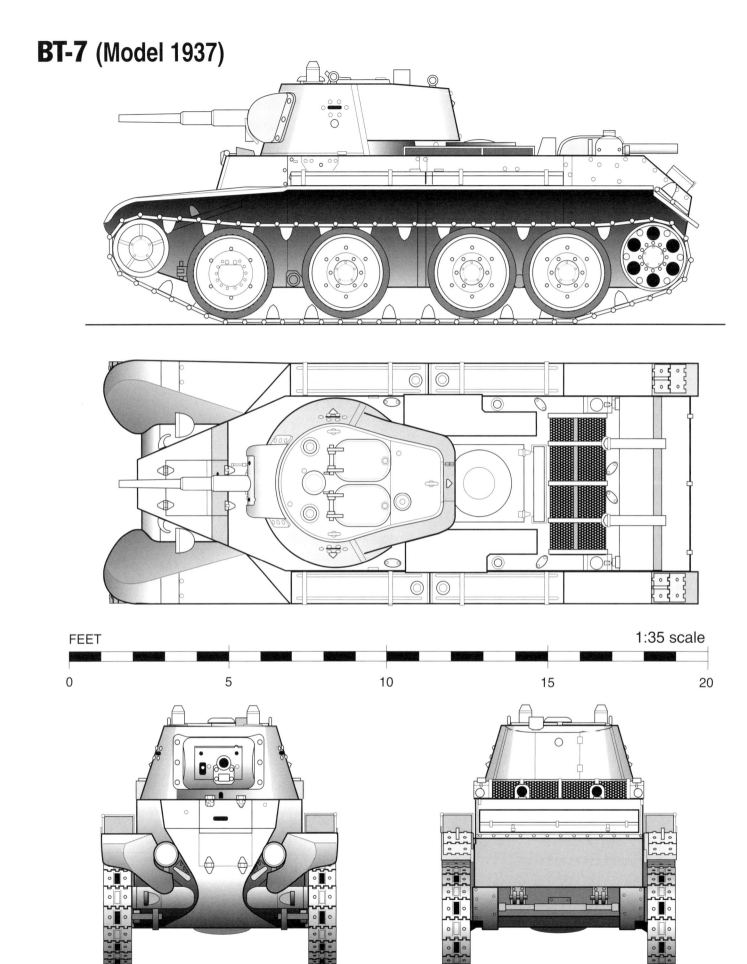

FEET

1:35 scale

0　　　　　　5　　　　　　10　　　　　　15　　　　　　20

T-40 Amphibious Light Tank
(Model 1940)

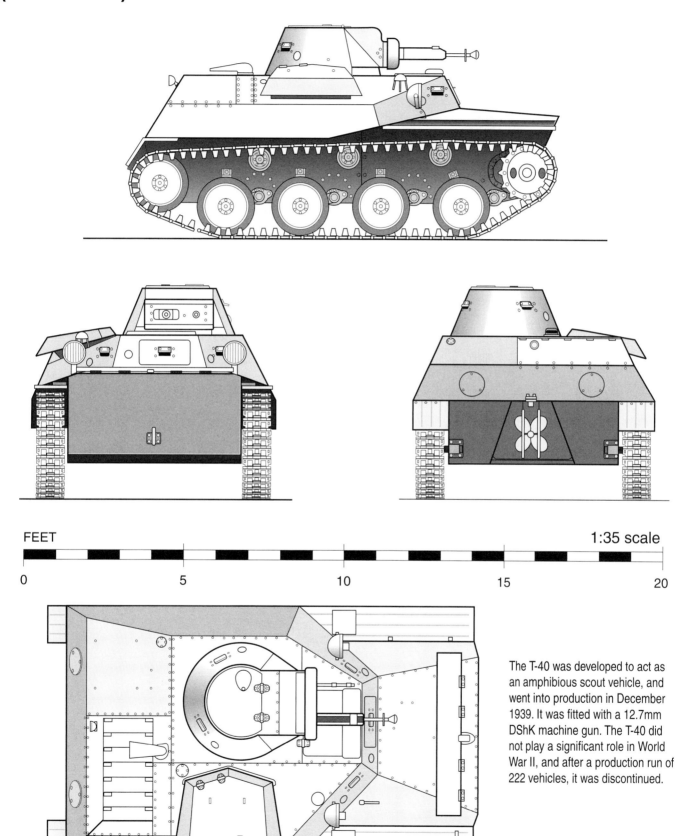

FEET

1:35 scale

0   5   10   15   20

The T-40 was developed to act as an amphibious scout vehicle, and went into production in December 1939. It was fitted with a 12.7mm DShK machine gun. The T-40 did not play a significant role in World War II, and after a production run of 222 vehicles, it was discontinued.

T-34/76 Model 1940

early production w. L-11 gun
and welded turret

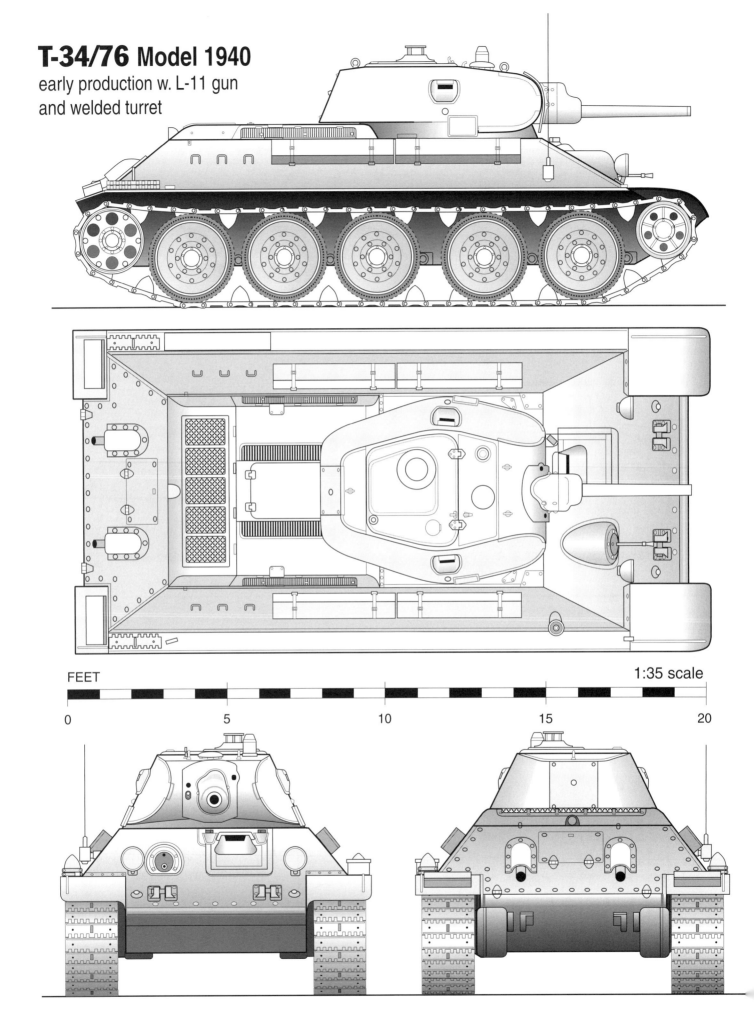

FEET

1:35 scale

0   5   10   15   20

Two photos of the early T-34 Model 1940 with the L-11 gun. As can be seen here, the upper photo shows the cast turret version, and the lower shot depicts the rolled homogeneous plate turret.

KV-2 Model 1939

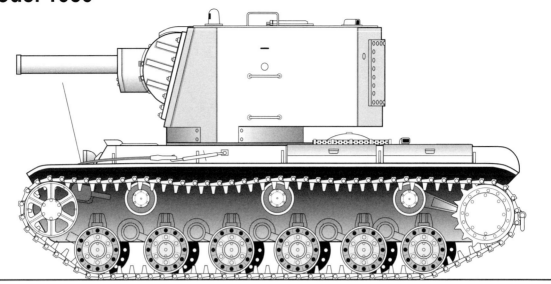

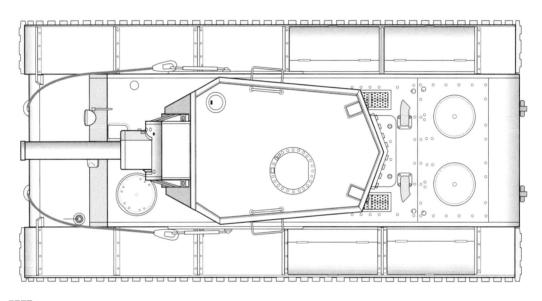

FEET

0   5   10   15   20

1:48 scale

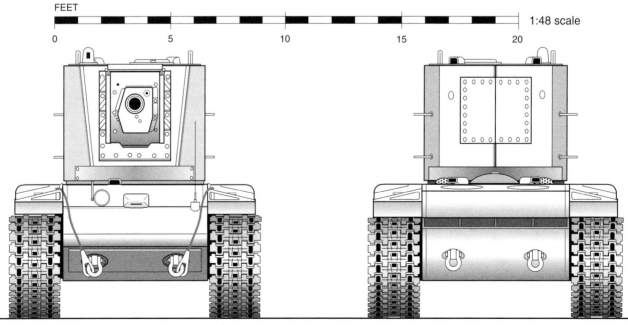

A great shot of a late version KV-2.

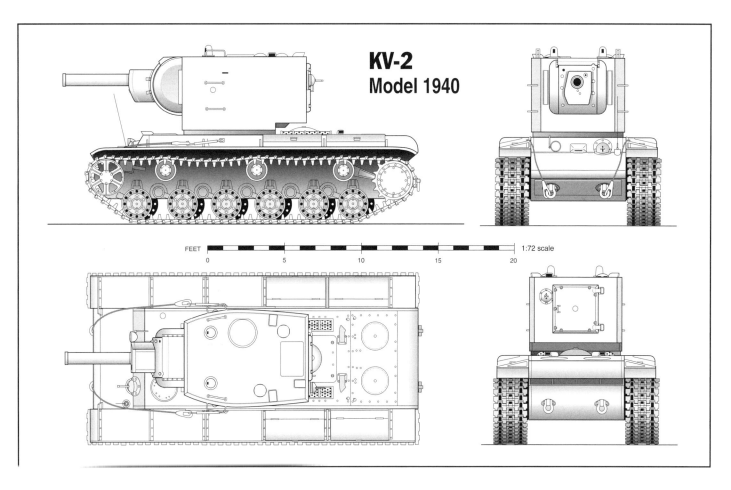

KV-2
Model 1940

FEET   1:72 scale
0   5   10   15   20

KV-2 Model 1940

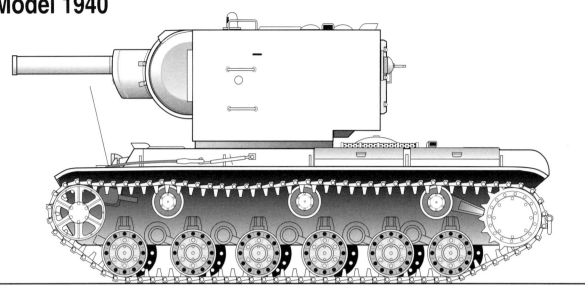

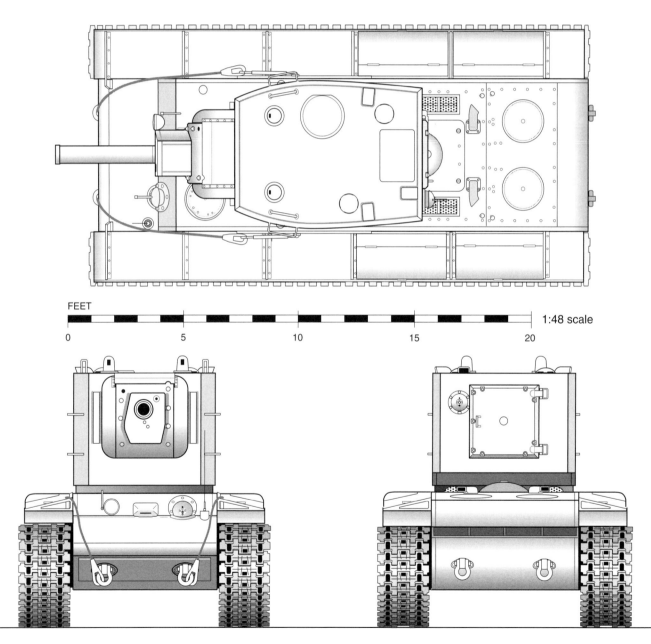

FEET

0   5   10   15   20

1:48 scale

BA-6 Model 1938
Medium Armored Car

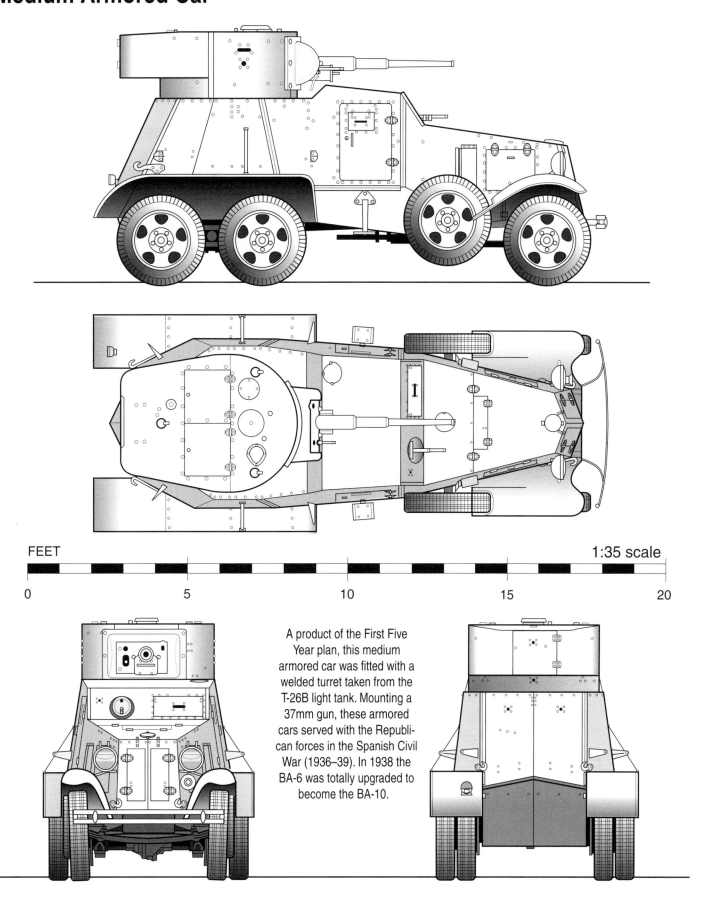

FEET   1:35 scale

0   5   10   15   20

A product of the First Five Year plan, this medium armored car was fitted with a welded turret taken from the T-26B light tank. Mounting a 37mm gun, these armored cars served with the Republican forces in the Spanish Civil War (1936–39). In 1938 the BA-6 was totally upgraded to become the BA-10.

KV-1 Model 1941

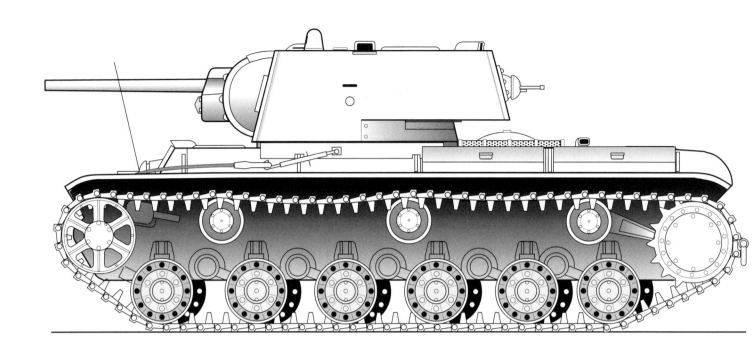

FEET

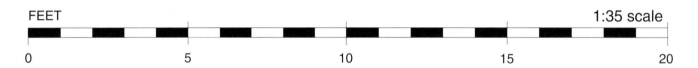

1:35 scale

0   5   10   15   20

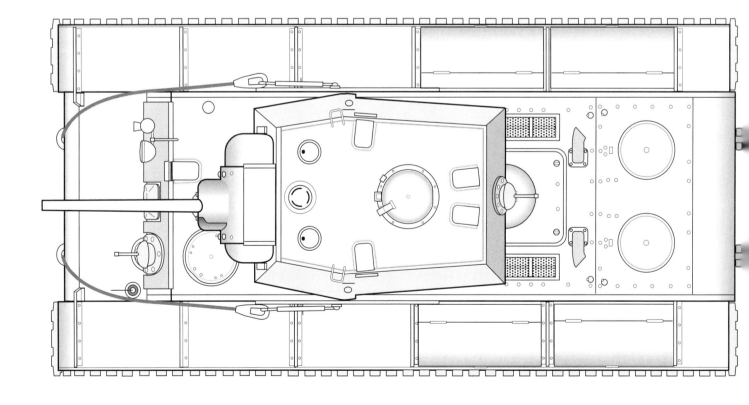

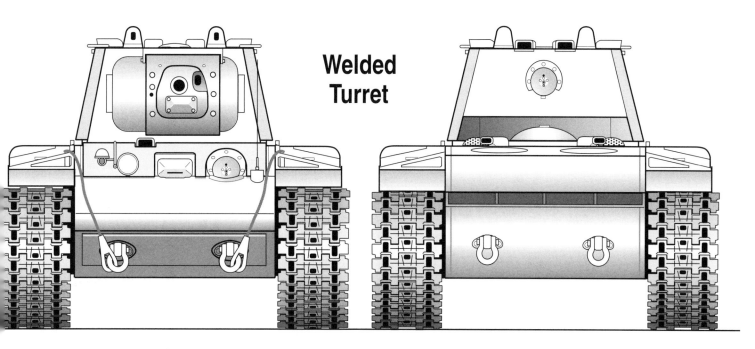

Welded Turret

A badly battered KV-1 knocked out in the early fighting in Russia. It is interesting to note that the main gun barrel has also been struck by an armor-piercing round.

KV-1 Model 1941

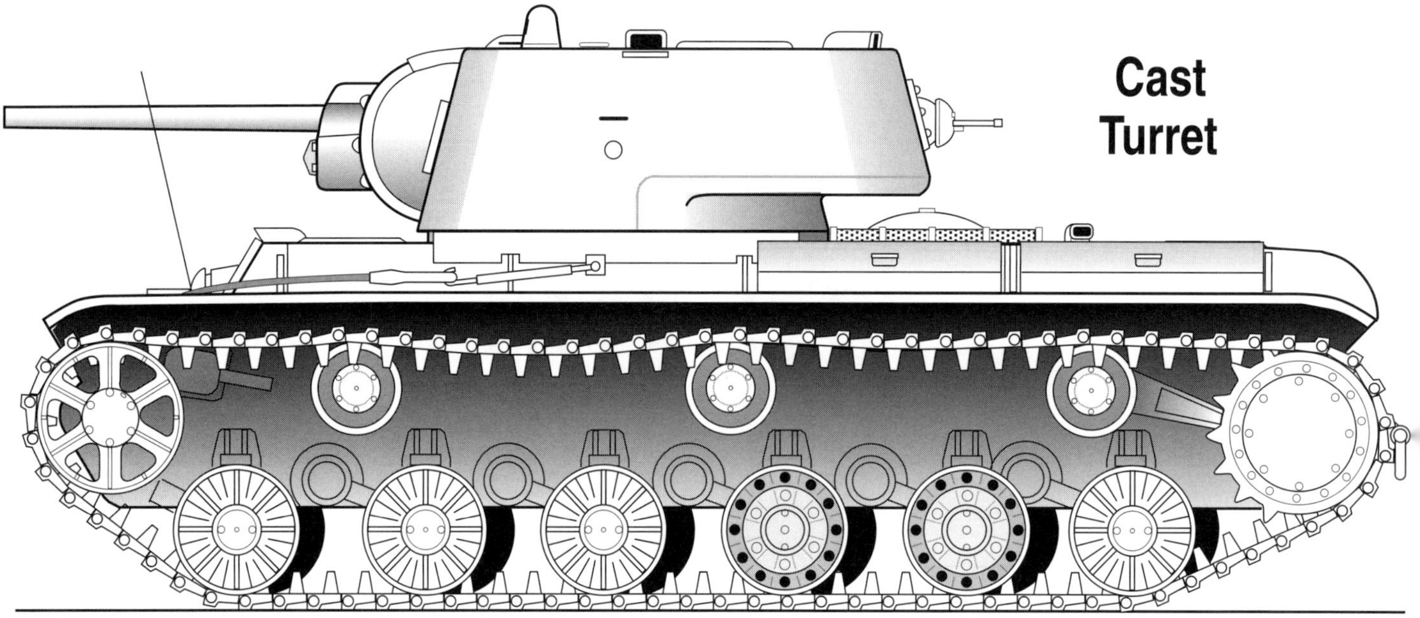
Cast
Turret

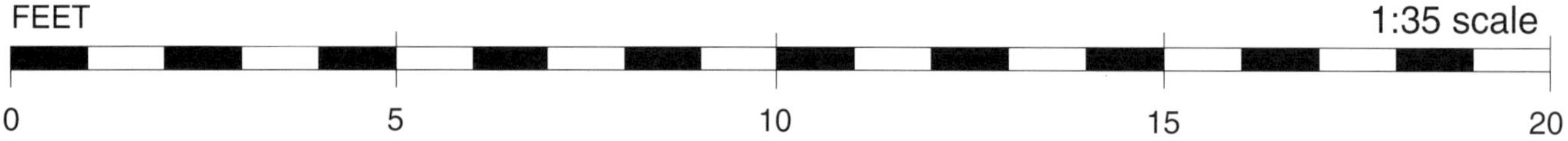
FEET
1:35 scale
0
5
10
15
20

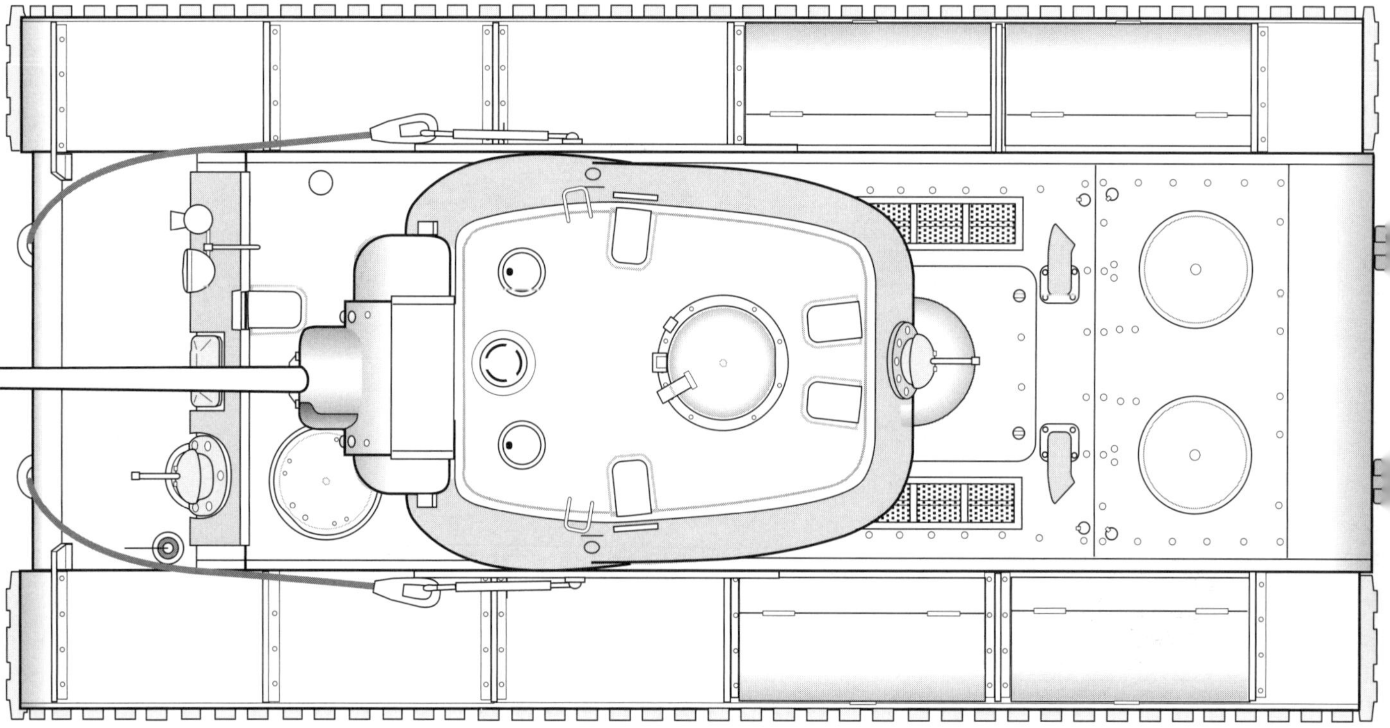

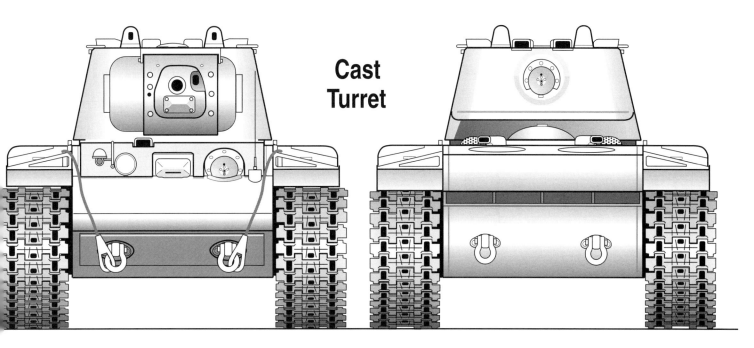

Cast Turret

A high-angle rear view of the exhaust system and the clean lines of the rear deck of a KV-1. Also easily seen here are the fender supports, although the rear stowage boxes have been removed.

T-60 Light Tank (Model 1941)

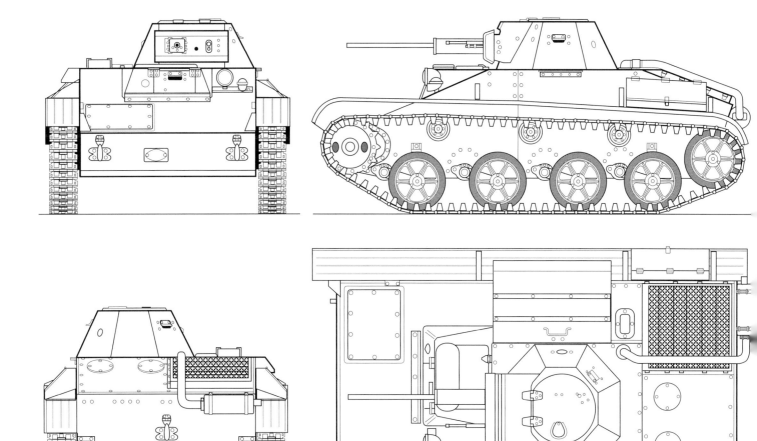

FEET

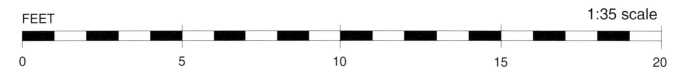

0   5   10   15   20

1:35 scale

T-60 Light Tank (Model 1942)

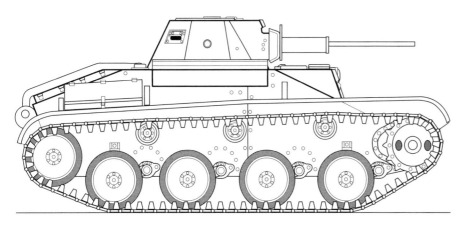

When World War II began, the Soviets had small numbers of their new T-40 amphibious scout tank available for reconnaissance roles, and the T-60 was just coming into production. By September 1941 the T-60 was acknowledged as the main Russian light tank, and began to replace the vehicles lost in the early fighting.

The early T-60 Model 1941 version featured spoked roadwheels and rear idlers, but the later Model 1942 went over to a simpler solid-disc type. Armor thickness was increased on this later model, but aside from this the two vehicles were almost identical. Its TNSh 20mm gun was far from effective on the battlefield, and its cross-country speed was to slow to keep abreast of the T-34s. However, it was kept in production, mainly because of a desperate need for new tanks. In late 1942, after over 6,000 had been built, production was halted in favor of the improved T-70.

T-34/76
Model 1942/43

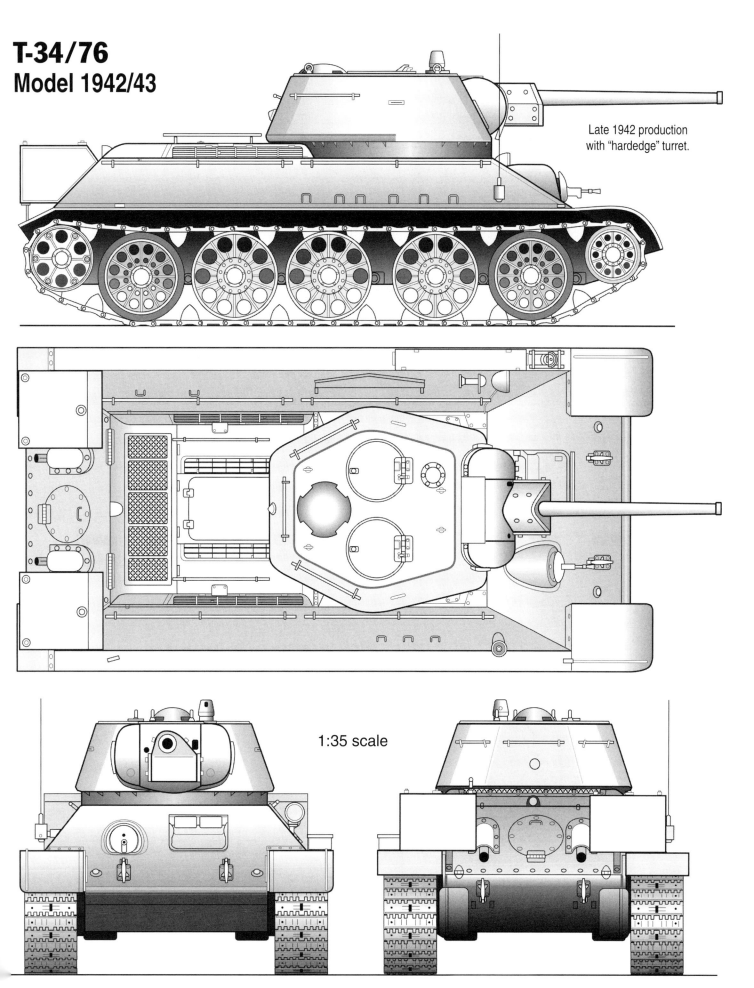

Late 1942 production with "hardedge" turret.

1:35 scale

KV-1 s Ekranami (with metal screens)

1940 turret with bolted appliqué armor and F-32 gun

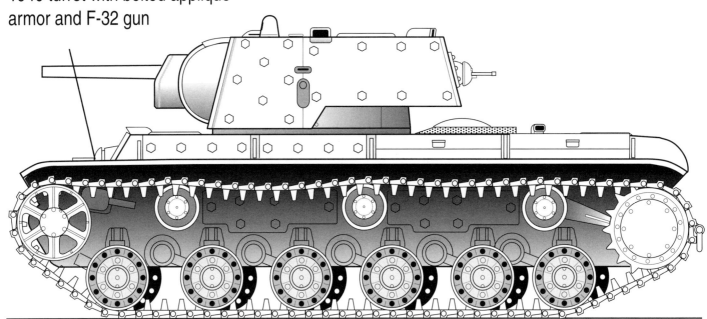

In April 1941 the Russians began applying appliqué armor plates to the turret and hull sides of their Model 1940 KV-1 heavy tanks. Even earlier Model 1939 versions that were in for repair or upgunning from the L-11 gun were fitted with this extra layer of 35mm bolted plate.

Unfortunately, experience proved that the bolt holes weakened the turret sides enough to allow several consecutive large-caliber hits to shatter the turret sides.

FEET

1:35 scale

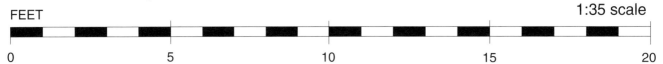

0   5   10   15   20

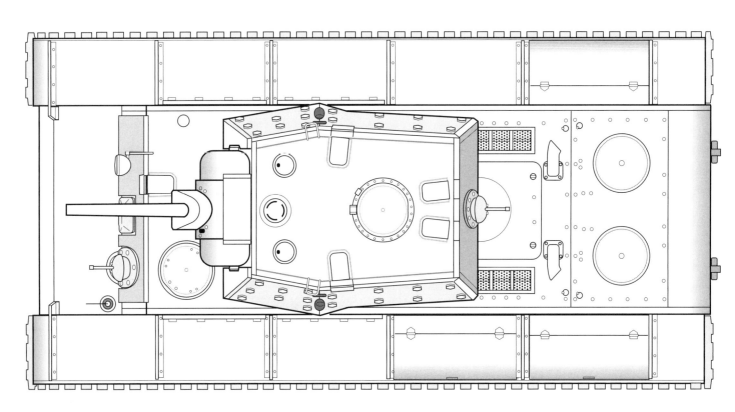

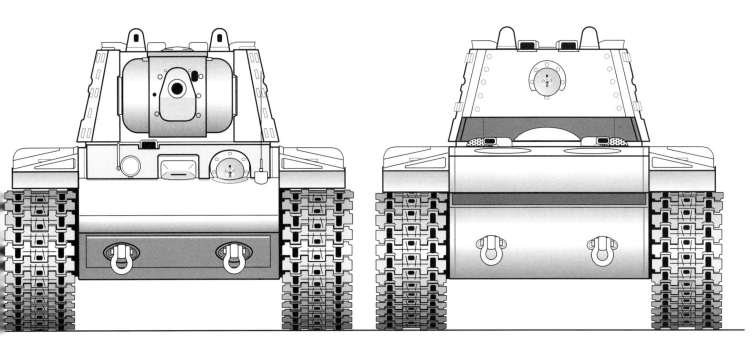

A front view of a Russian KV-1 Ekranami with the bolted-on turret appliqué armor.

T-34/76 Model 1943

1943 production with ChKZ turret.

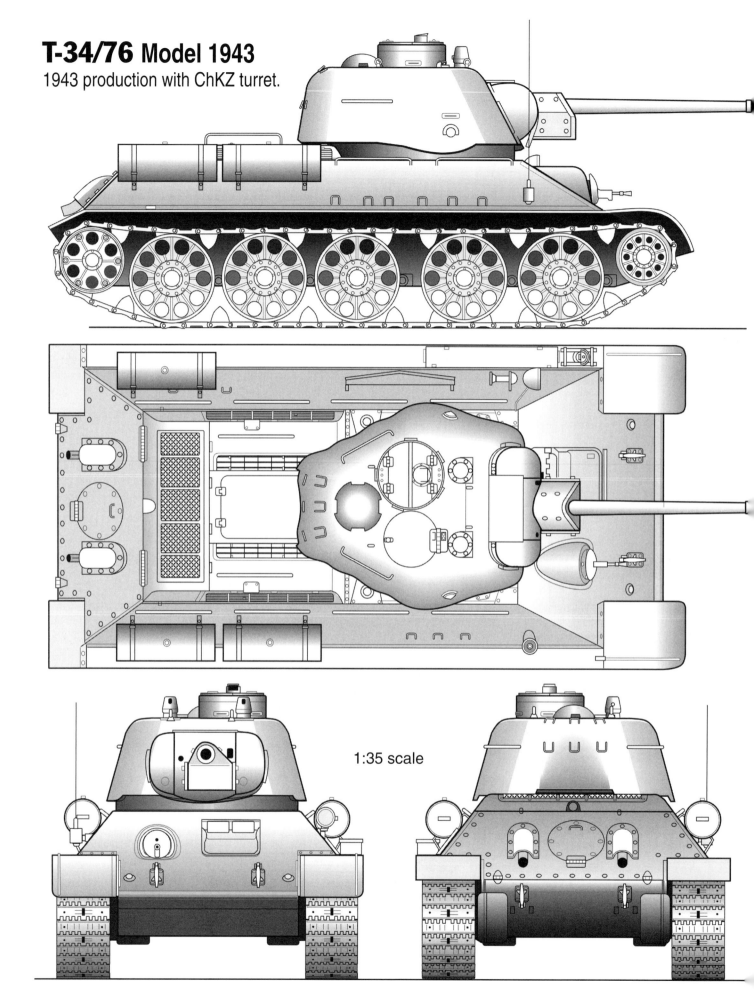

1:35 scale

Komsomolyets STZ-3 Armored Artillery Transporter

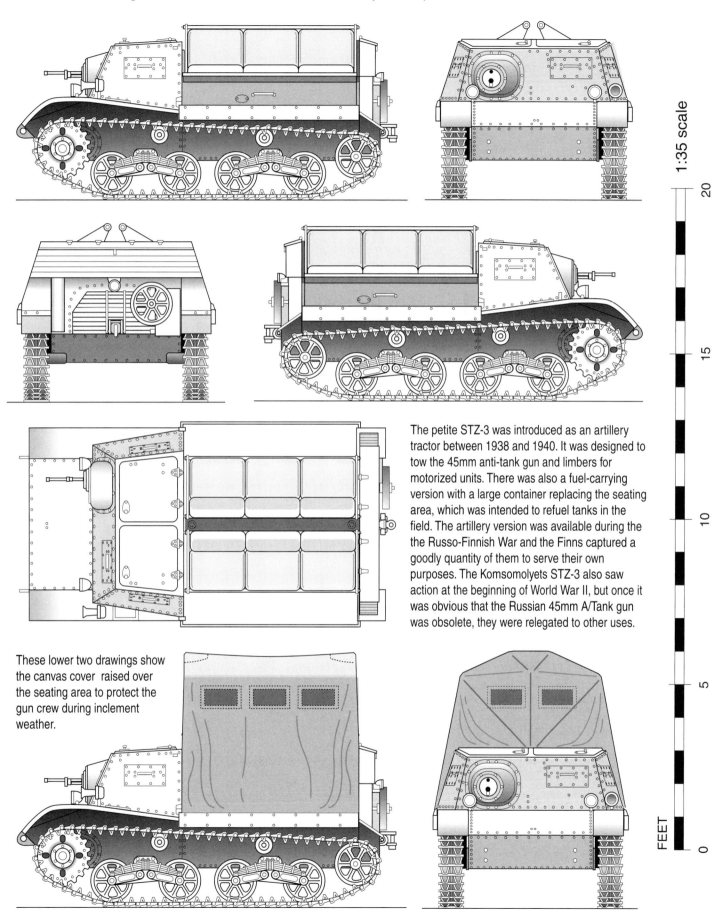

The petite STZ-3 was introduced as an artillery tractor between 1938 and 1940. It was designed to tow the 45mm anti-tank gun and limbers for motorized units. There was also a fuel-carrying version with a large container replacing the seating area, which was intended to refuel tanks in the field. The artillery version was available during the the Russo-Finnish War and the Finns captured a goodly quantity of them to serve their own purposes. The Komsomolyets STZ-3 also saw action at the beginning of World War II, but once it was obvious that the Russian 45mm A/Tank gun was obsolete, they were relegated to other uses.

These lower two drawings show the canvas cover raised over the seating area to protect the gun crew during inclement weather.

1:35 scale

20

15

10

5

FEET

0

KV-1s

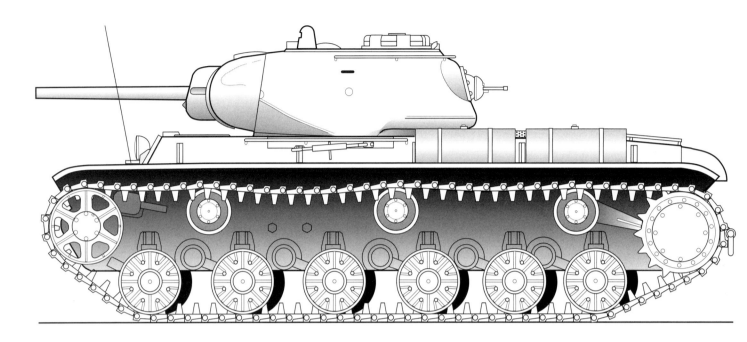

The original KV-1 proved to be too slow to work in conjunction with the faster T-34 mediums. To overcome this, a new lighter-armored design began to appear. These were designated as KV-1s, the "s"—for *skorostnoy*, or "fast"—denoting their faster speed.

FEET   1:35 scale

0   5   10   15   20

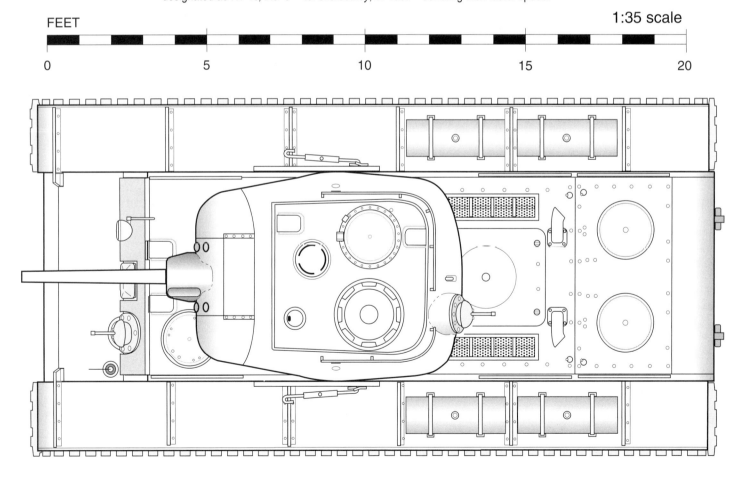

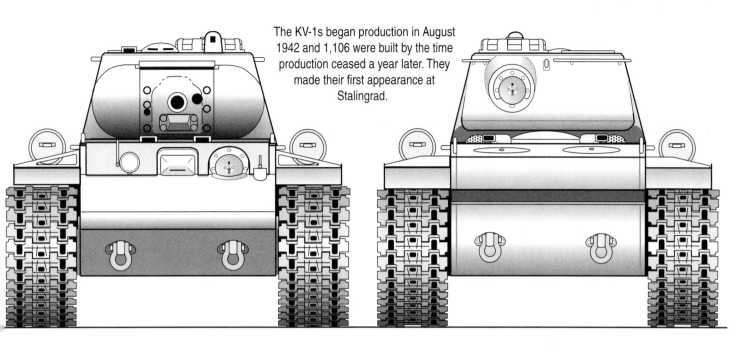

The KV-1s began production in August 1942 and 1,106 were built by the time production ceased a year later. They made their first appearance at Stalingrad.

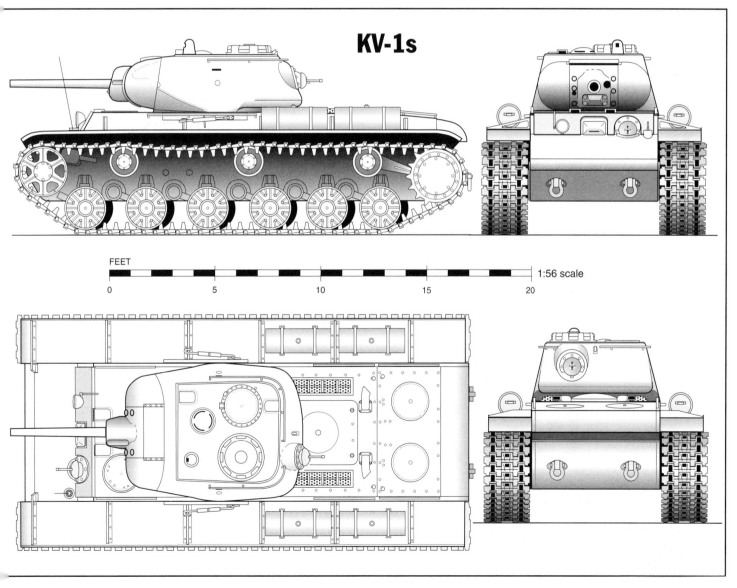

KV-1s

FEET

1:56 scale

0   5   10   15   20

SU-122 (Model 1943)

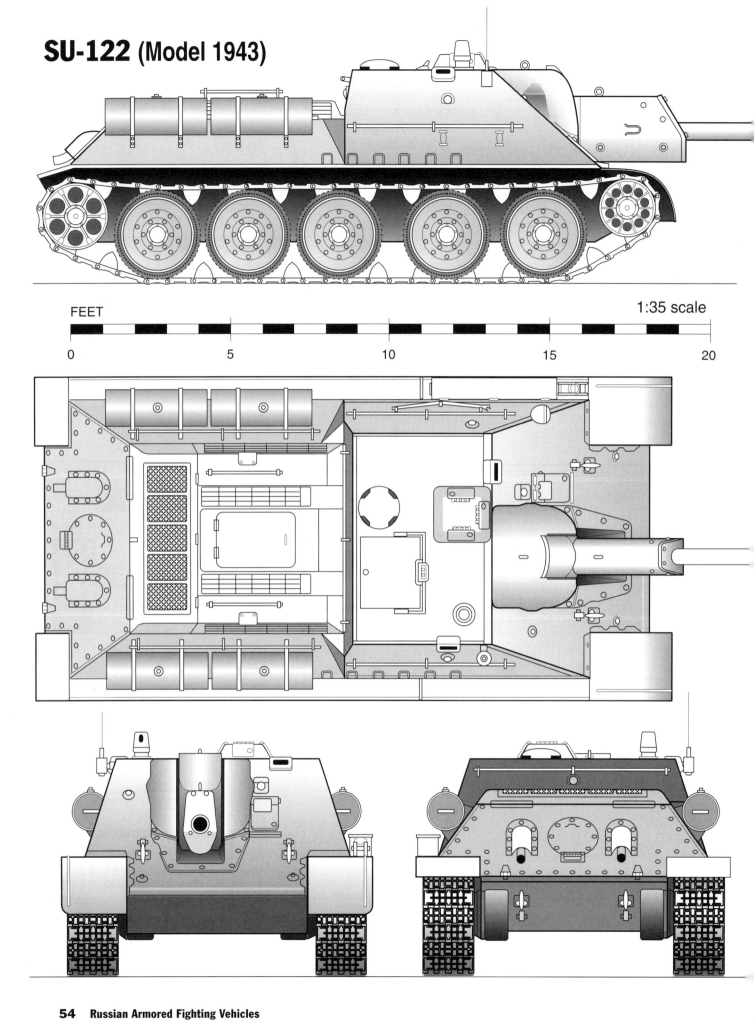

FEET

1:35 scale

0   5   10   15   20

KV-8 Flamethrower
with 45mm gun

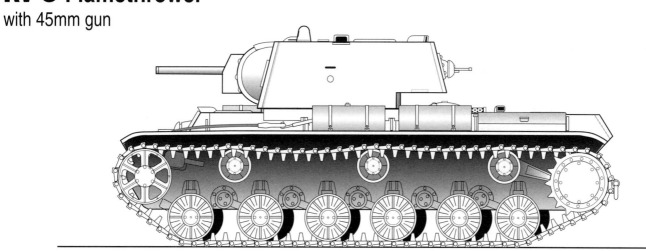

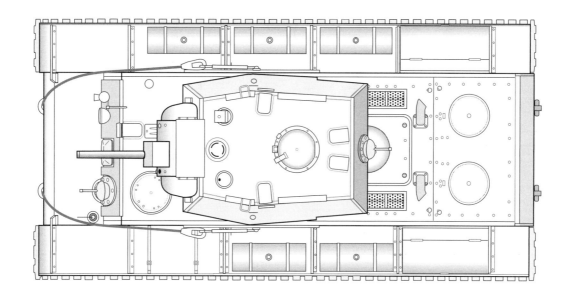

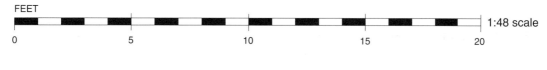

FEET

0   5   10   15   20

1:48 scale

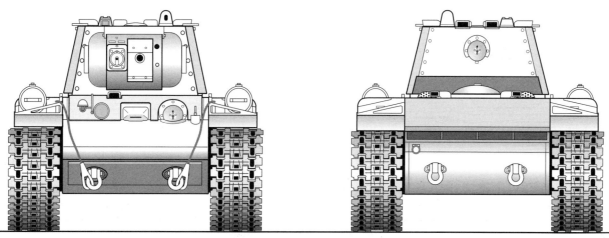

SU-76i

These vehicles were built on captured German Pz.Kpfw. III chassis.

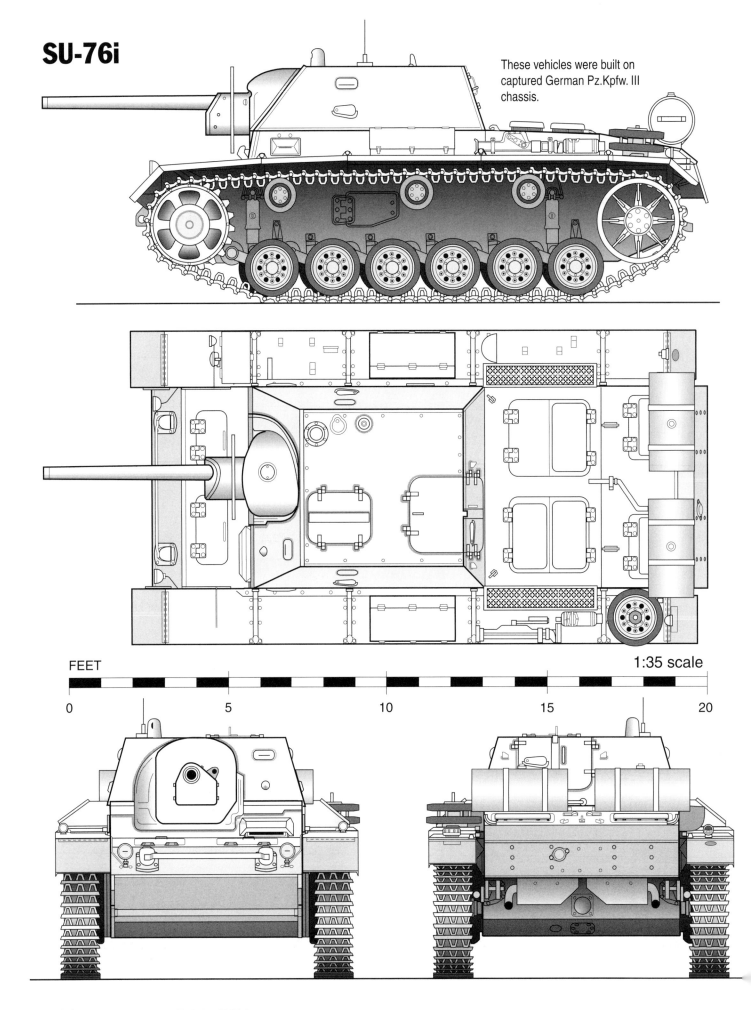

FEET

1:35 scale

0   5   10   15   20

BTR-40
Reconnaissance Scout
& Troop Carrier

FEET

1:35 scale

0   5   10   15   20

SU-152

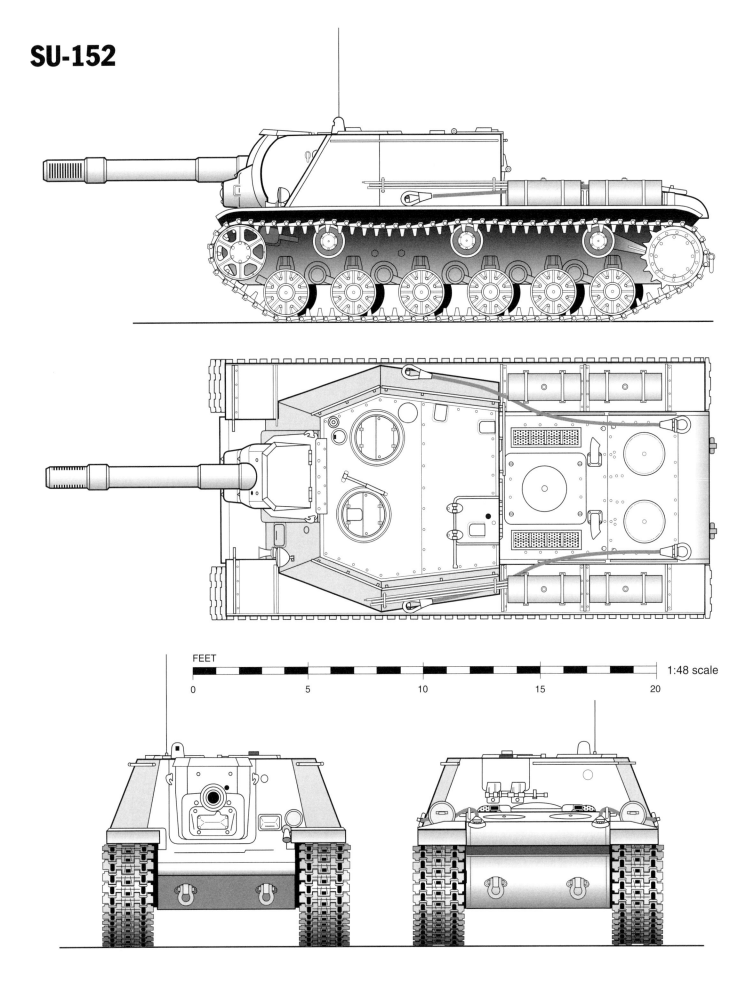

FEET

1:48 scale

0   5   10   15   20

ISU-122

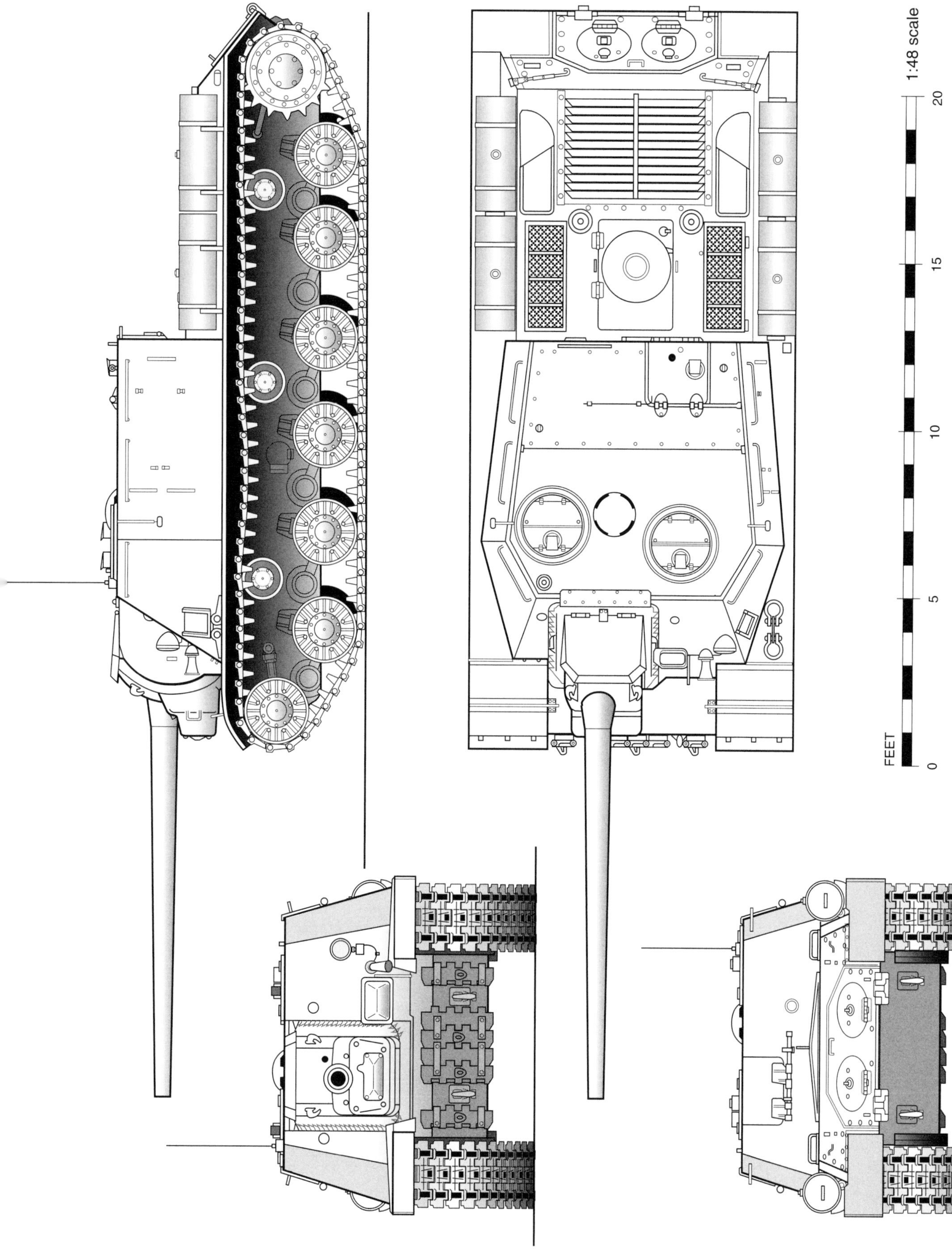
1:48 scale
FEET
0
5
10
15
20

KV-1C Model 1942
with ZiS-5/F-34 gun

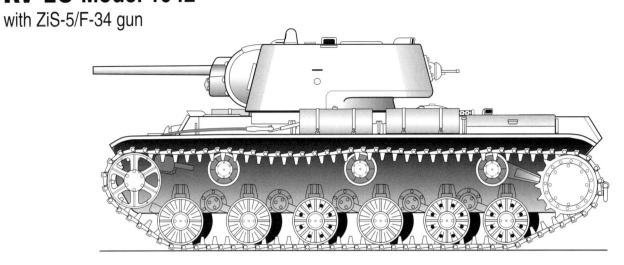

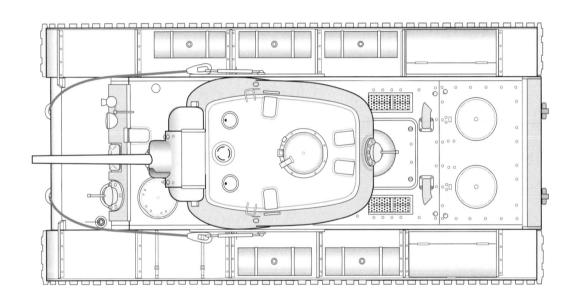

FEET
0   5   10   15   20
1:48 scale

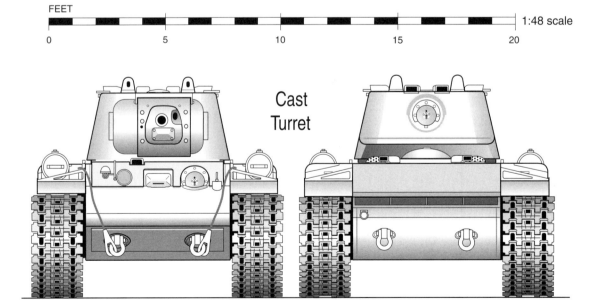

Cast
Turret

A group of KV-1C heavy tanks move forward during the 1943 battles in the Stalingrad area.

A good front view of a KV-1C on display in Russia showing the additional armor plate added to the bow.

ISU-152

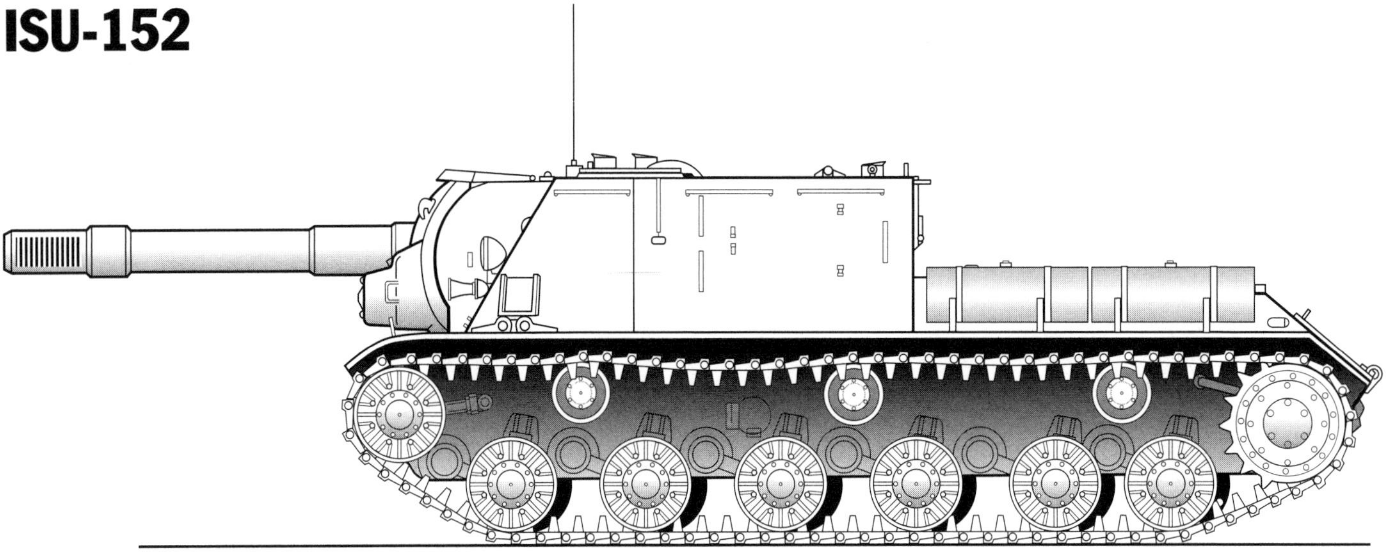

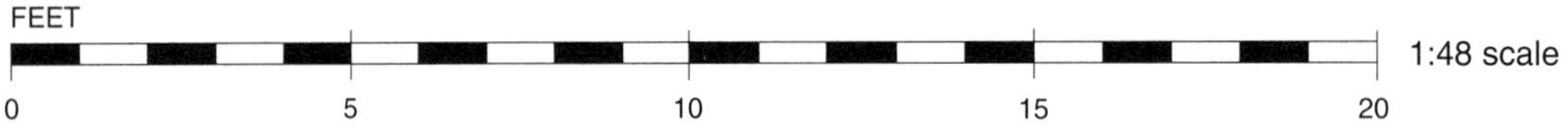
FEET
0
5
10
15
20
1:48 scale

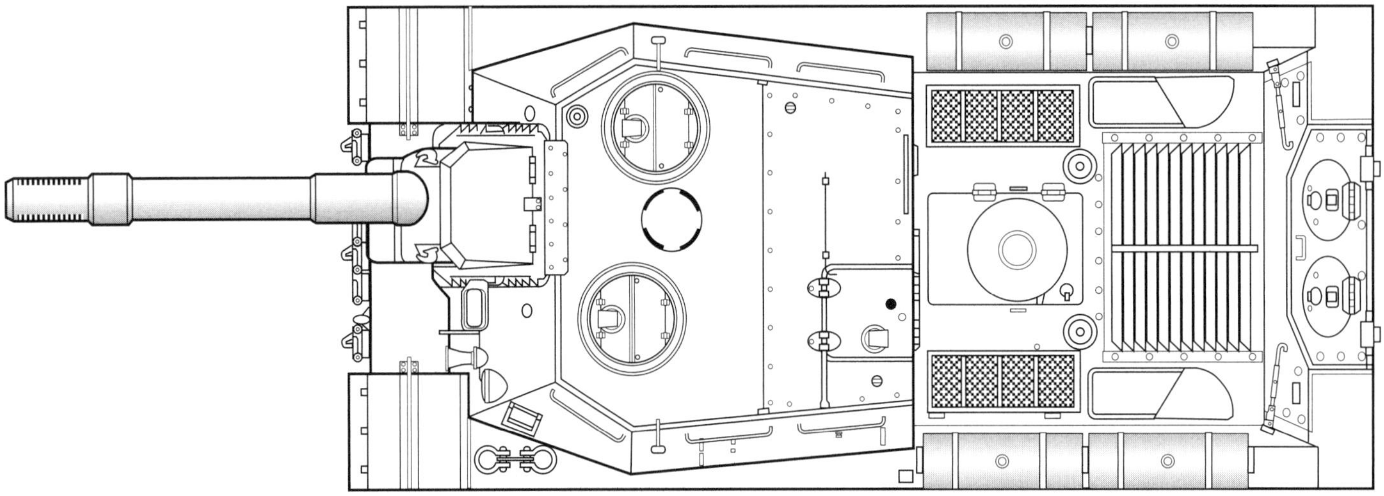

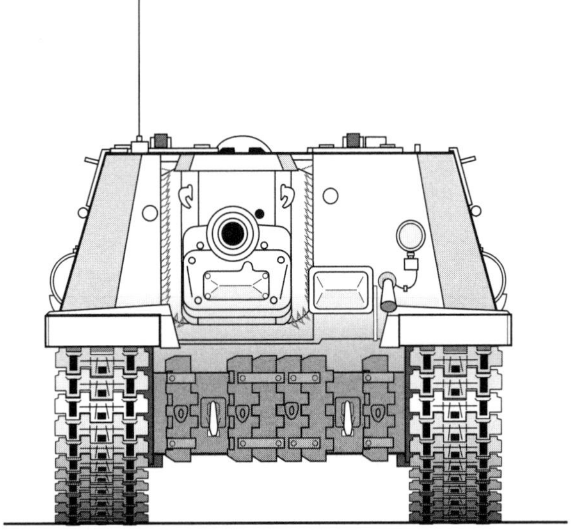

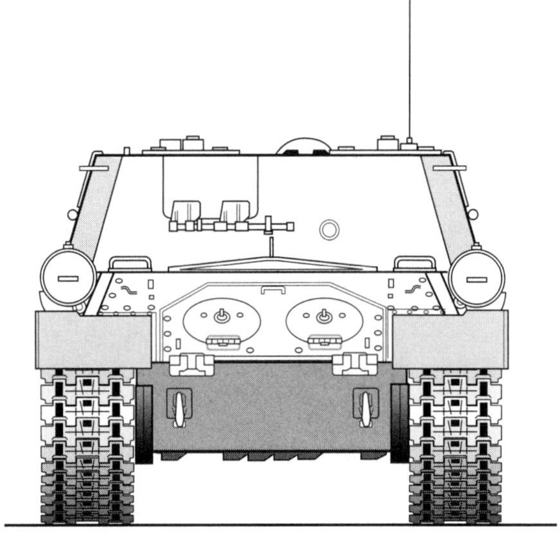

SU-76M

Early Model

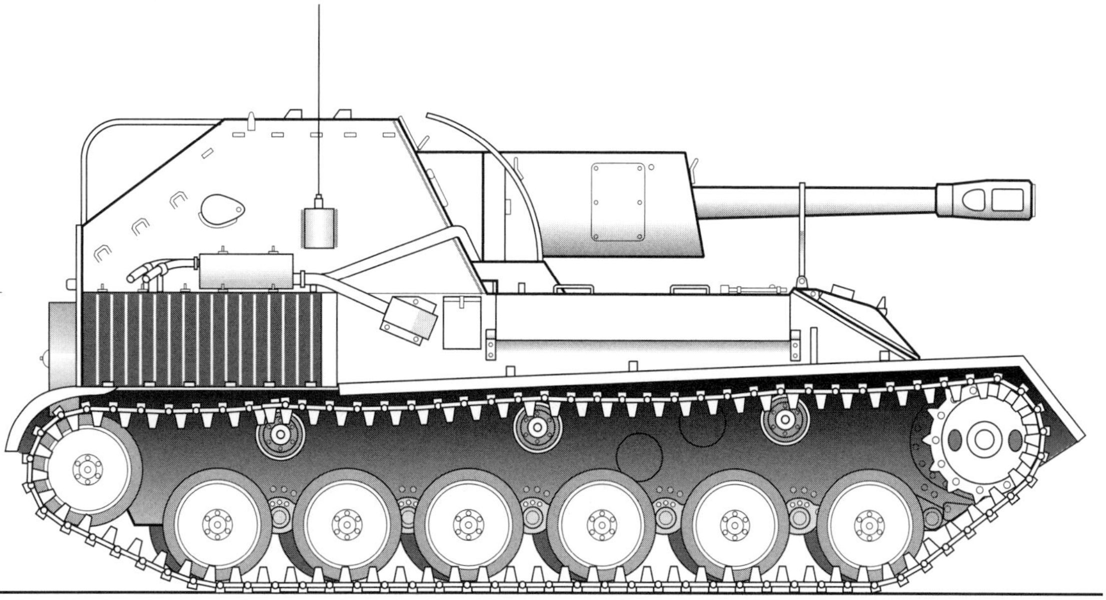

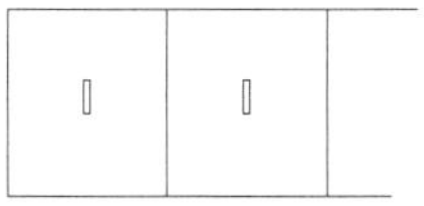

Three Severe Weather Panels like the above could be fitted over the side air intakes to keep out snow and other debris.

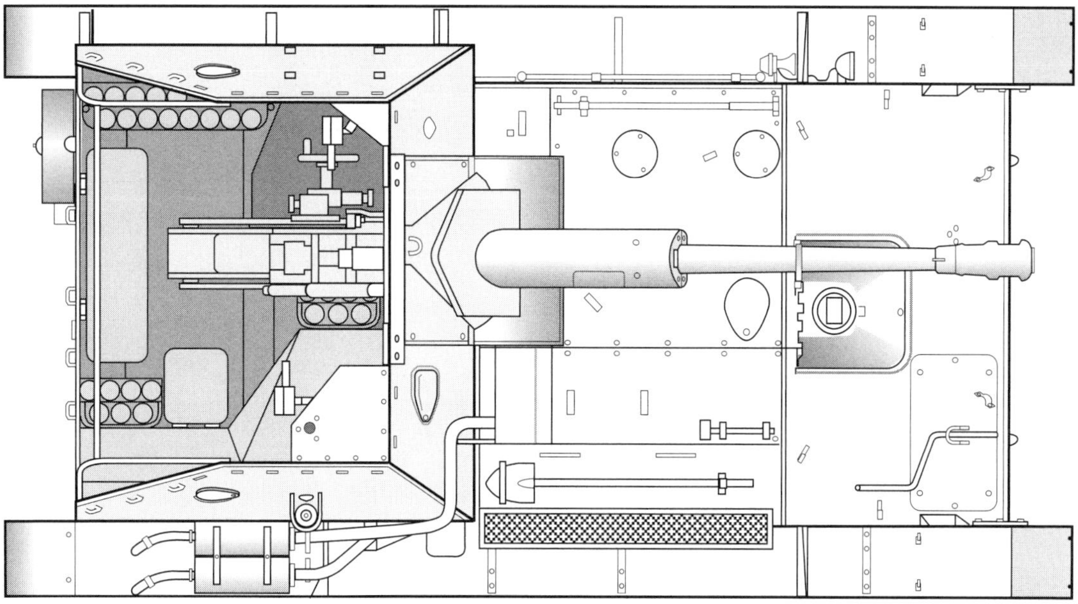

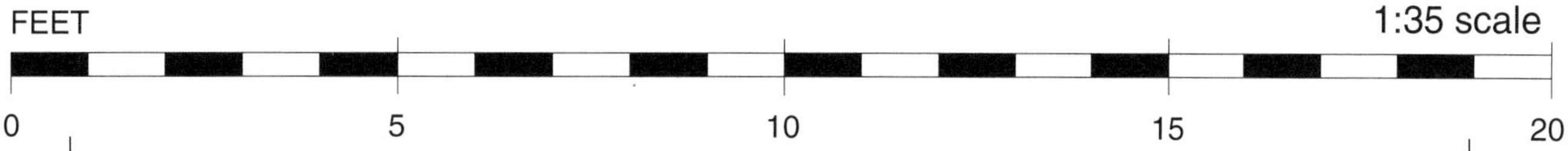
FEET
1:35 scale
0
5
10
15
20

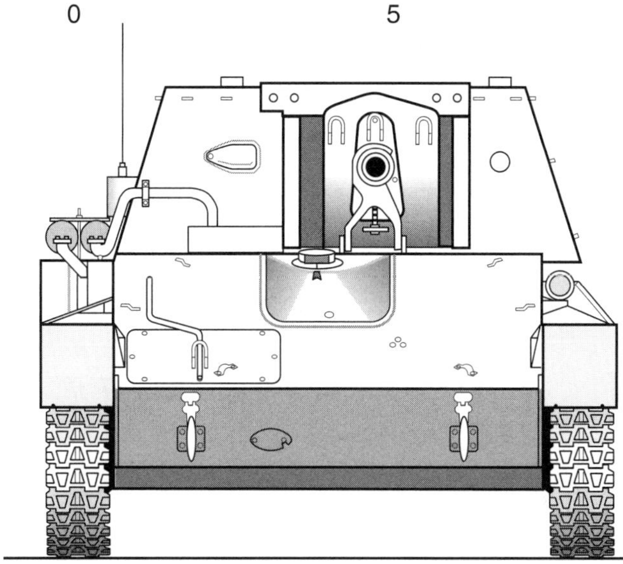

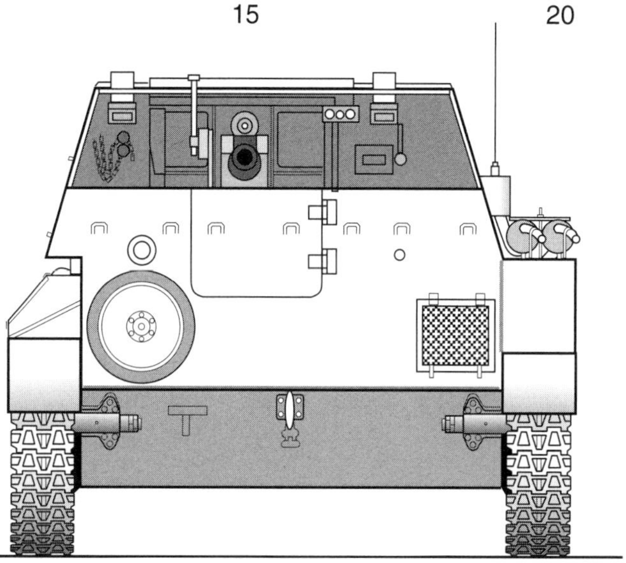

KV-85

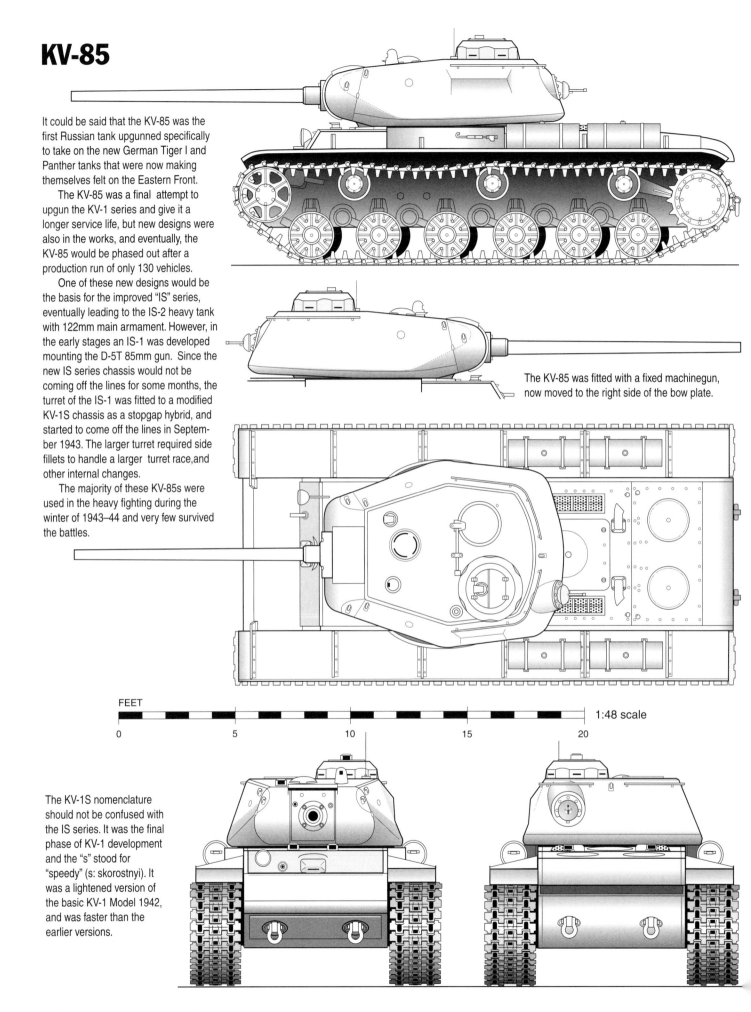

It could be said that the KV-85 was the first Russian tank upgunned specifically to take on the new German Tiger I and Panther tanks that were now making themselves felt on the Eastern Front.

The KV-85 was a final attempt to upgun the KV-1 series and give it a longer service life, but new designs were also in the works, and eventually, the KV-85 would be phased out after a production run of only 130 vehicles.

One of these new designs would be the basis for the improved "IS" series, eventually leading to the IS-2 heavy tank with 122mm main armament. However, in the early stages an IS-1 was developed mounting the D-5T 85mm gun. Since the new IS series chassis would not be coming off the lines for some months, the turret of the IS-1 was fitted to a modified KV-1S chassis as a stopgap hybrid, and started to come off the lines in September 1943. The larger turret required side fillets to handle a larger turret race, and other internal changes.

The majority of these KV-85s were used in the heavy fighting during the winter of 1943–44 and very few survived the battles.

The KV-85 was fitted with a fixed machinegun, now moved to the right side of the bow plate.

FEET

0   5   10   15   20

1:48 scale

The KV-1S nomenclature should not be confused with the IS series. It was the final phase of KV-1 development and the "s" stood for "speedy" (s: skorostnyi). It was a lightened version of the basic KV-1 Model 1942, and was faster than the earlier versions.

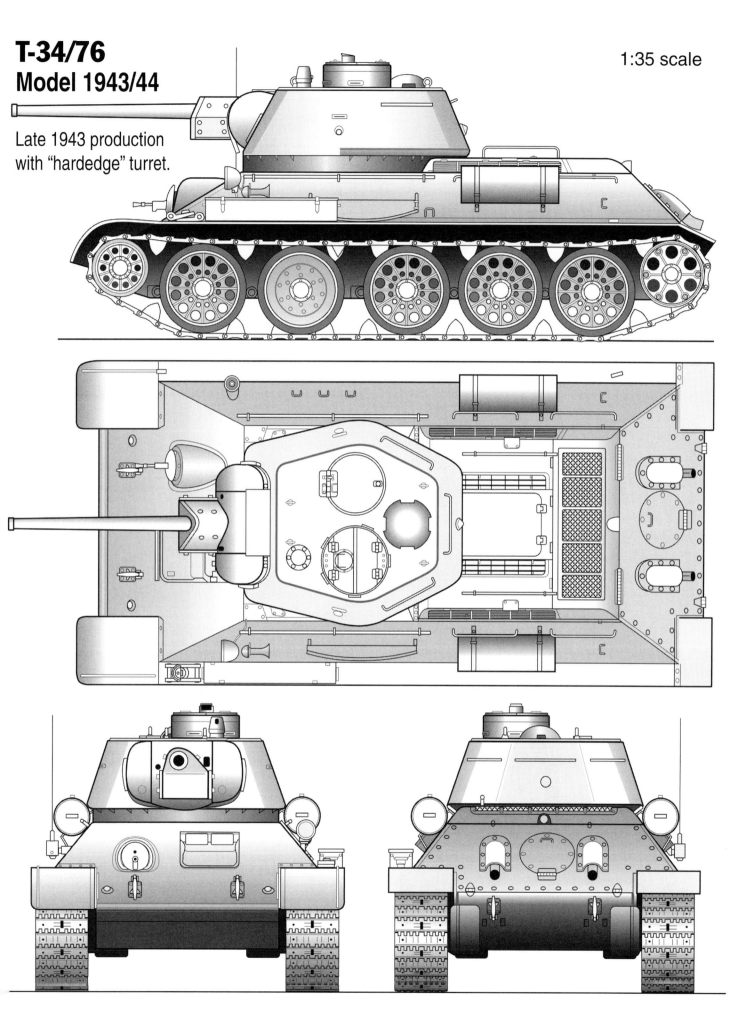

T-34/76
Model 1943/44

Late 1943 production
with "hardedge" turret.

1:35 scale

SU-76M
Late Model

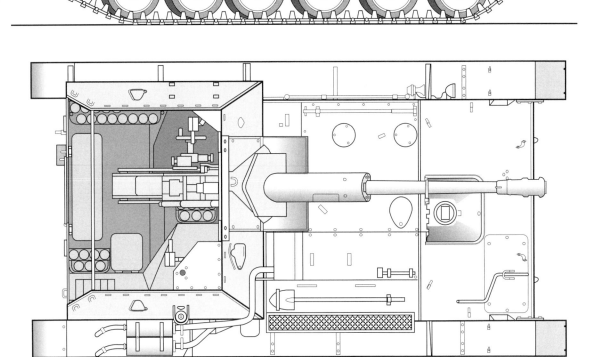

Three Severe Weather Panels like the above could be fitted over the side air intakes to keep out snow and other debris.

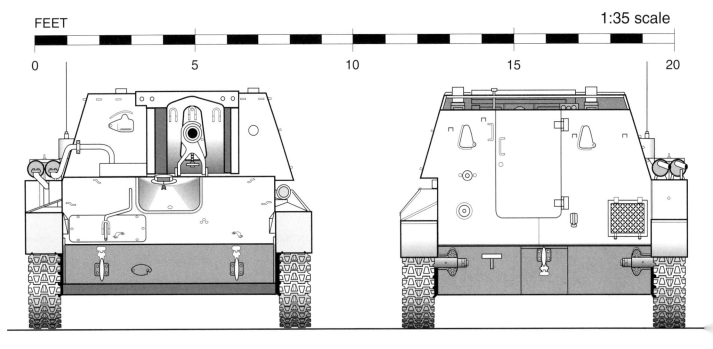

FEET

1:35 scale

0	5	10	15	20

Clear front and side view close-ups of a late SU-76 on display in Russia.

ZIS-42 Half-Track
(1942–1944)

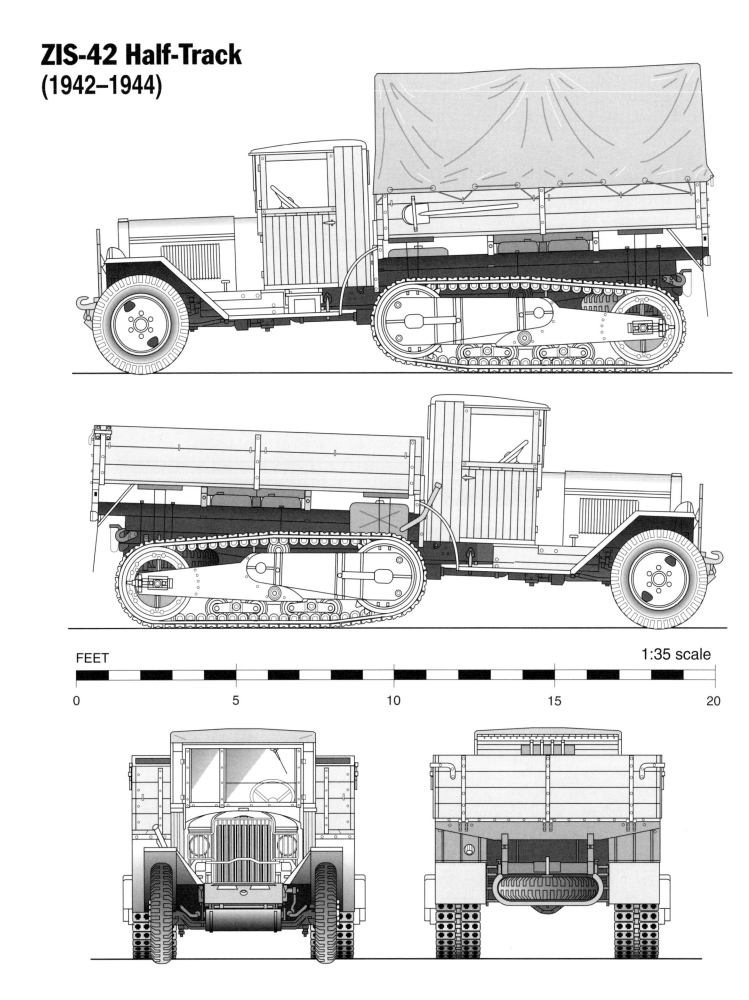

FEET

1:35 scale

0   5   10   15   20

T-50 Light Tank

(Maly Klim) little Klim

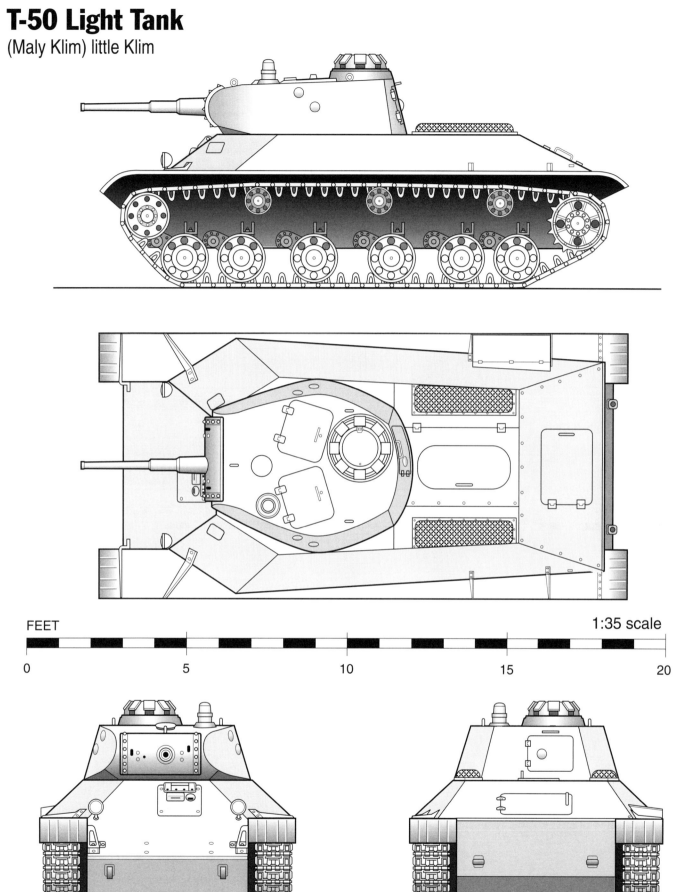

FEET

1:35 scale

0   5   10   15   20

SU-85

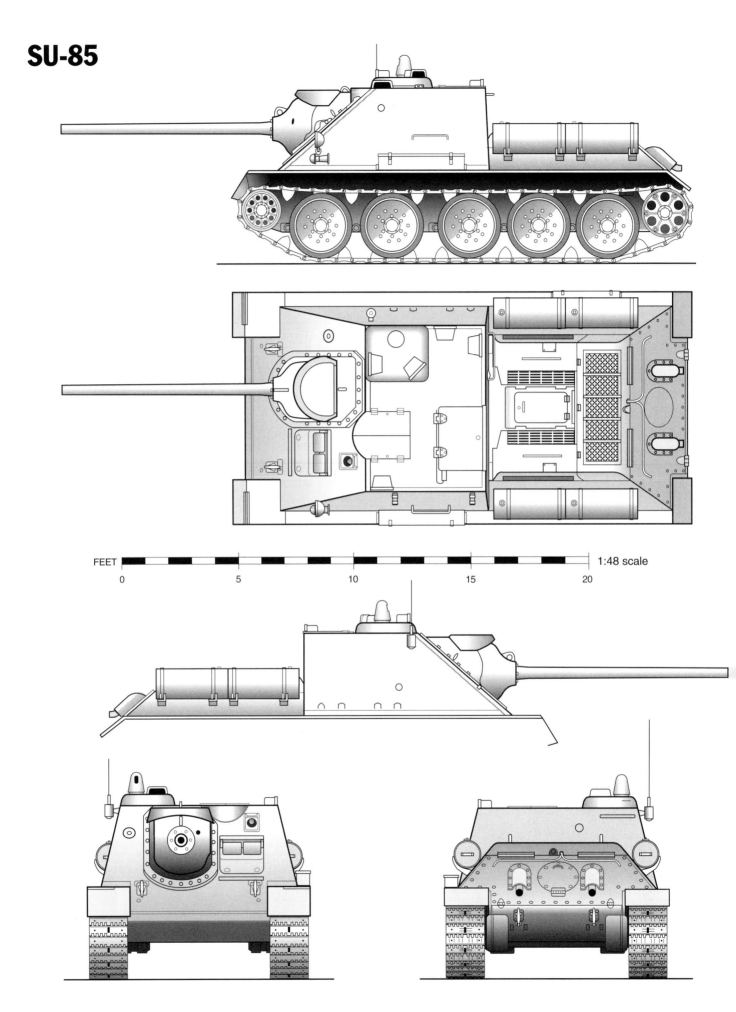

FEET

1:48 scale

0   5   10   15   20

A great shot of a captured Russian SU-85 in the hands of its German captors. These captured vehicles were referred to as "Beutepanzer" and were distinguished by their oversize Balkenkreuz.

An interesting high-angle view of the rear deck of the SU-100 tank destroyer. The most obvious distinguishing features between it and the SU-85 are the larger gun and the protruding cupola on the right front of the fighting compartment.

SU-100

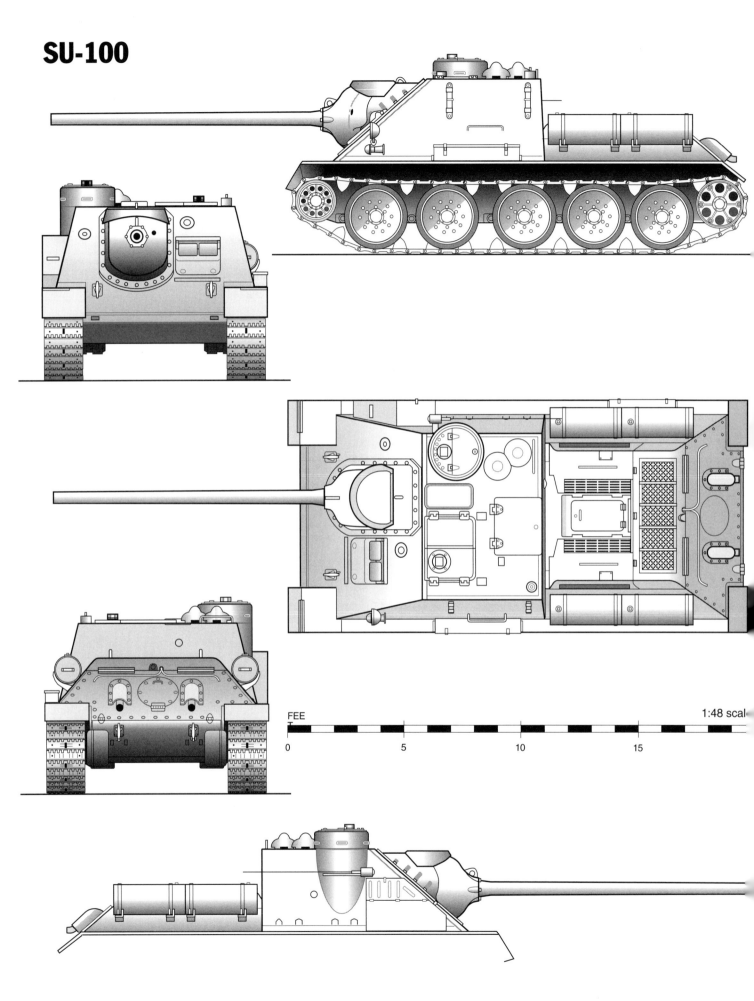

FEET

0   5   10   15

1:48 scal

VT-34 ARV

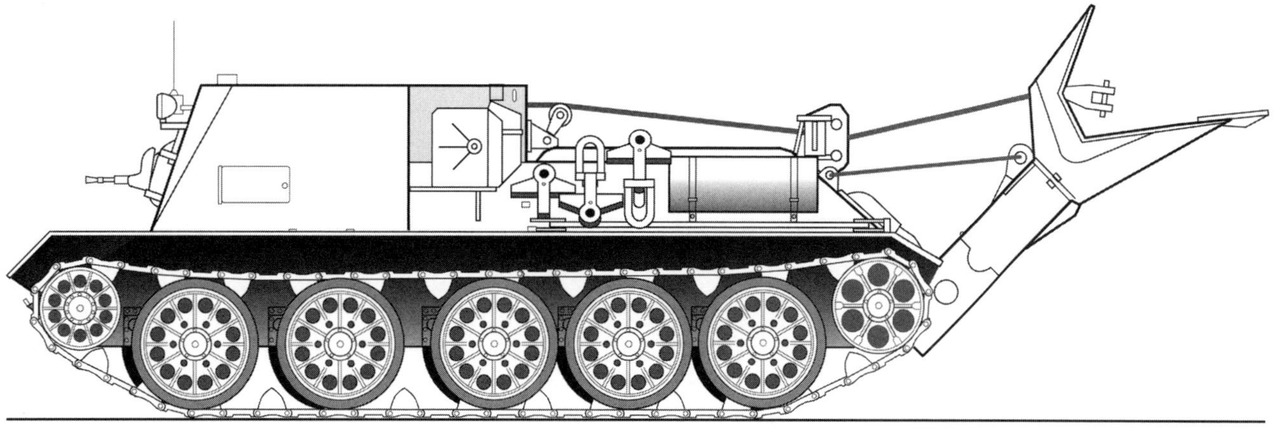

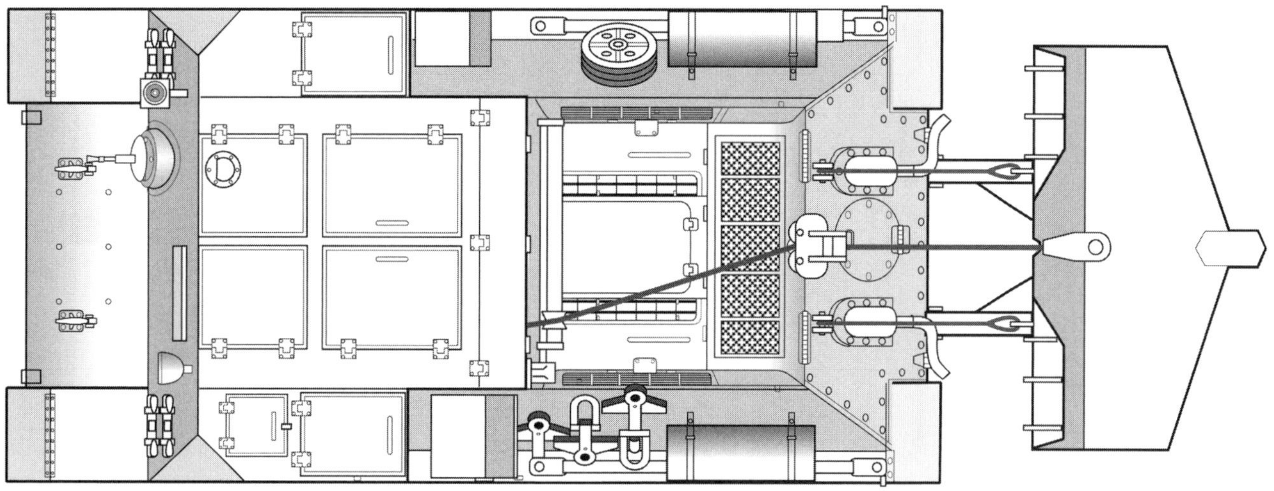

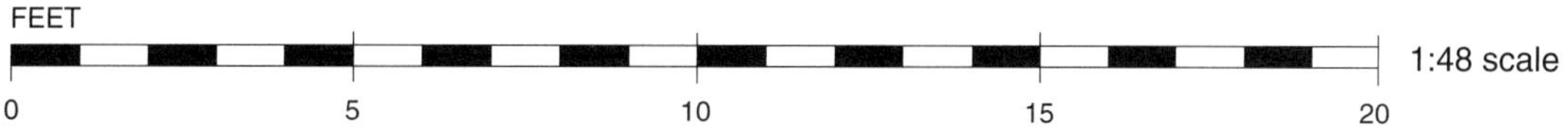
FEET
0
5
10
15
20
1:48 scale

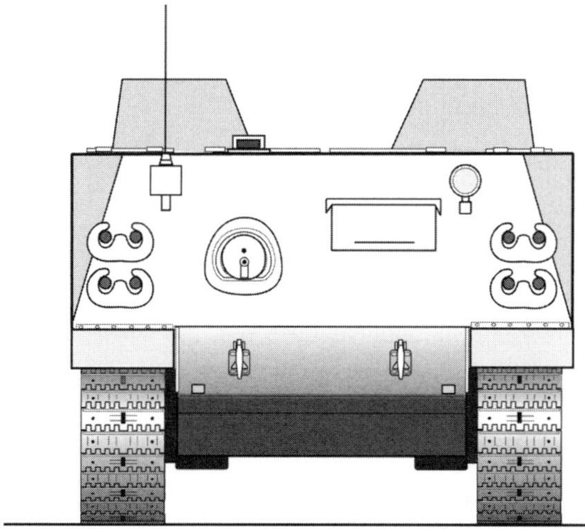

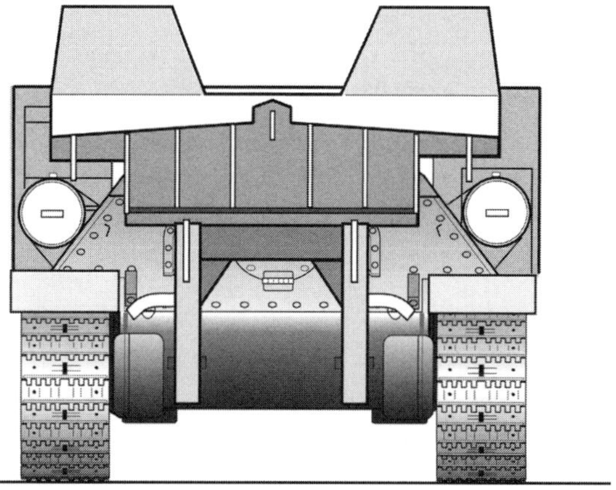

IS-2m Model 1944

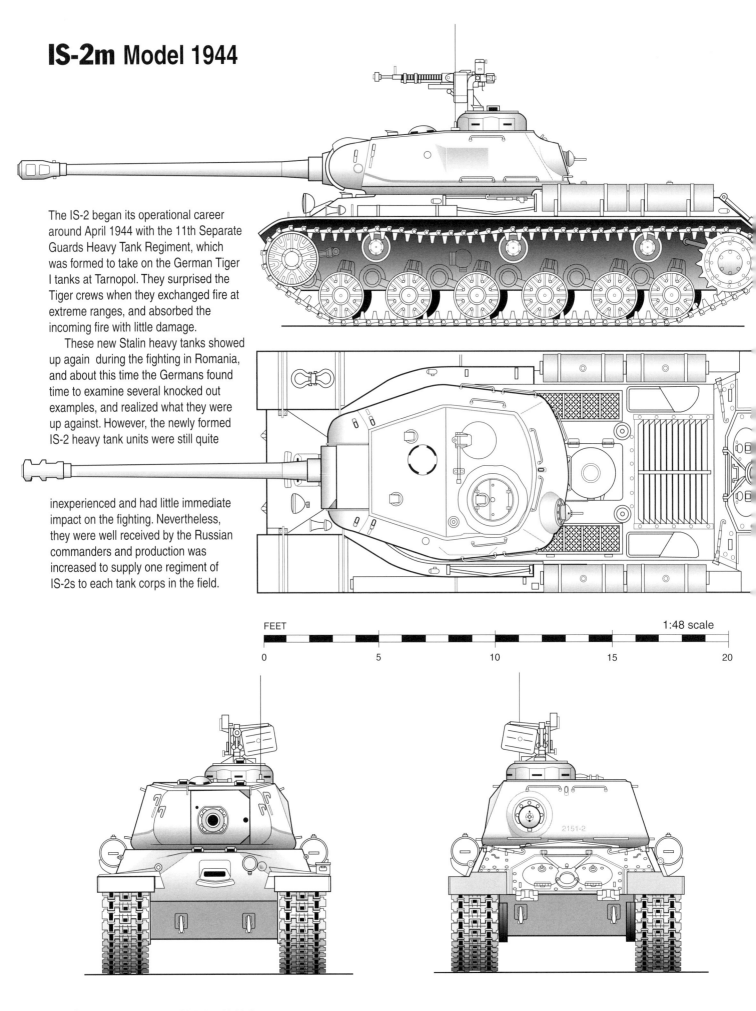

The IS-2 began its operational career around April 1944 with the 11th Separate Guards Heavy Tank Regiment, which was formed to take on the German Tiger I tanks at Tarnopol. They surprised the Tiger crews when they exchanged fire at extreme ranges, and absorbed the incoming fire with little damage.

These new Stalin heavy tanks showed up again during the fighting in Romania, and about this time the Germans found time to examine several knocked out examples, and realized what they were up against. However, the newly formed IS-2 heavy tank units were still quite

inexperienced and had little immediate impact on the fighting. Nevertheless, they were well received by the Russian commanders and production was increased to supply one regiment of IS-2s to each tank corps in the field.

FEET   1:48 scale

0   5   10   15   20

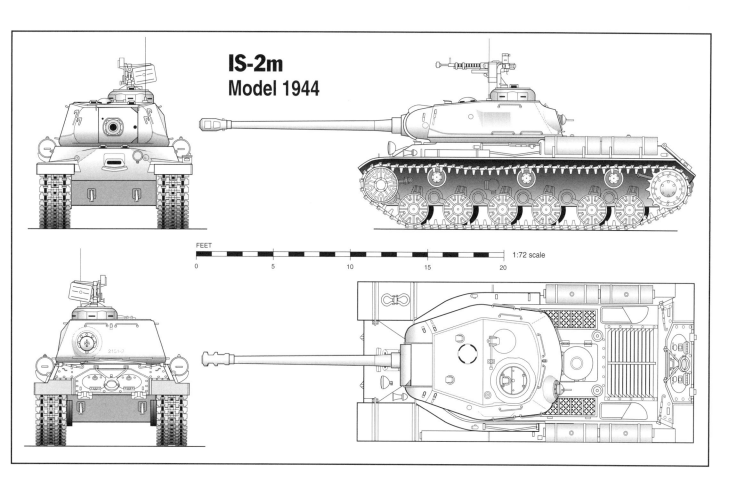

IS-2m
Model 1944

FEET

1:72 scale

One of the few remaining IS-2 heavy tanks on display at the Kubinka tank museum, north of Moscow.

T-34/85

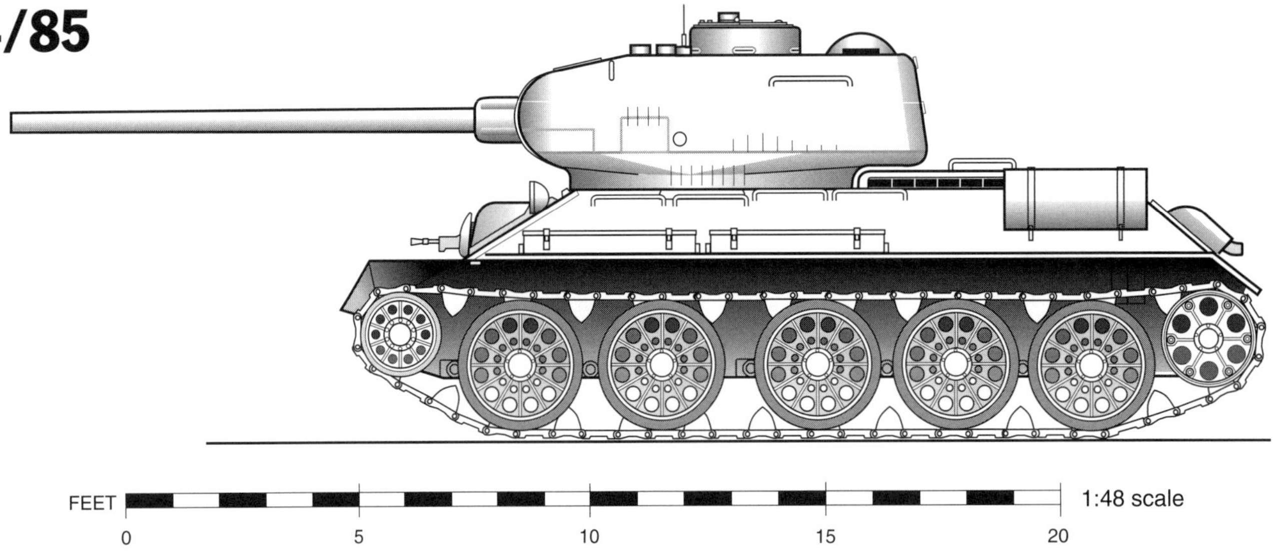
FEET
0
5
10
15
20
1:48 scale

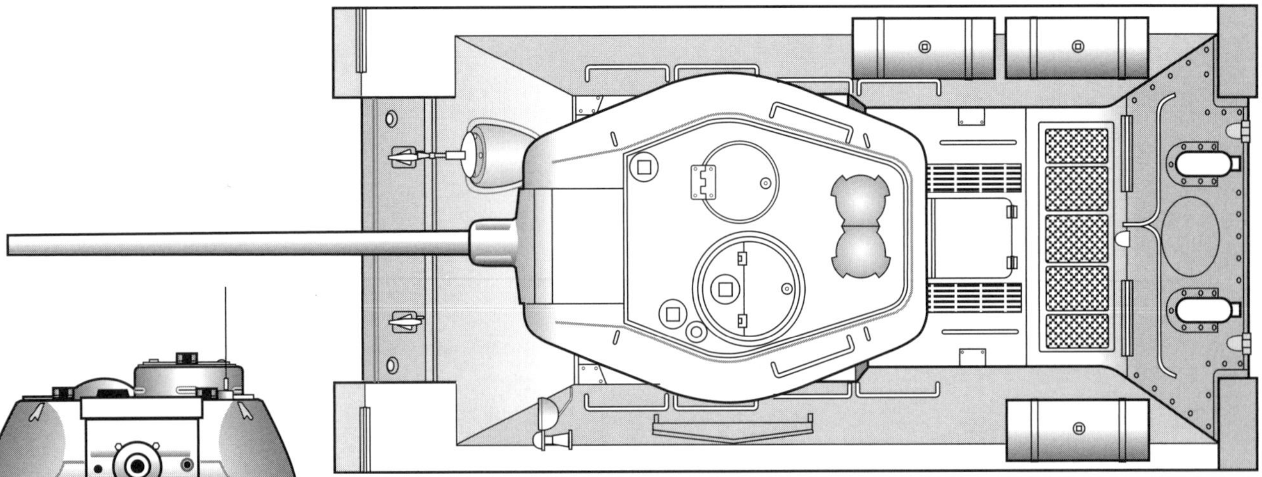

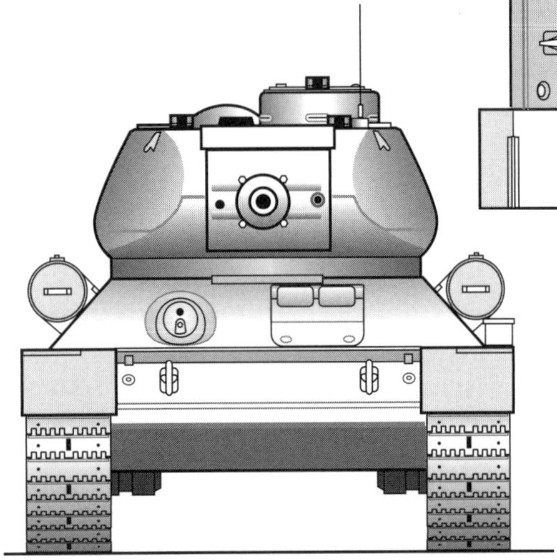

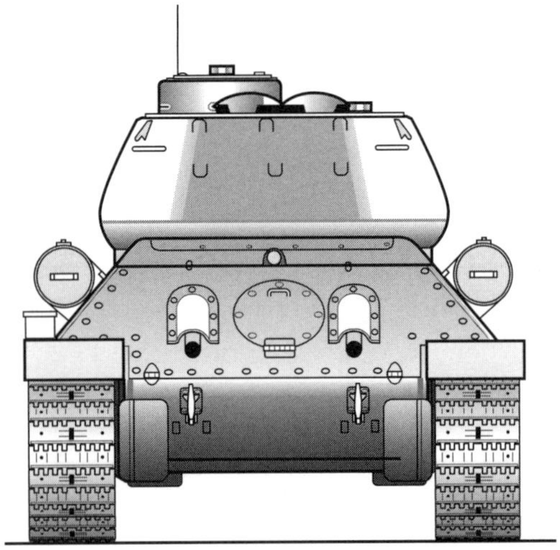

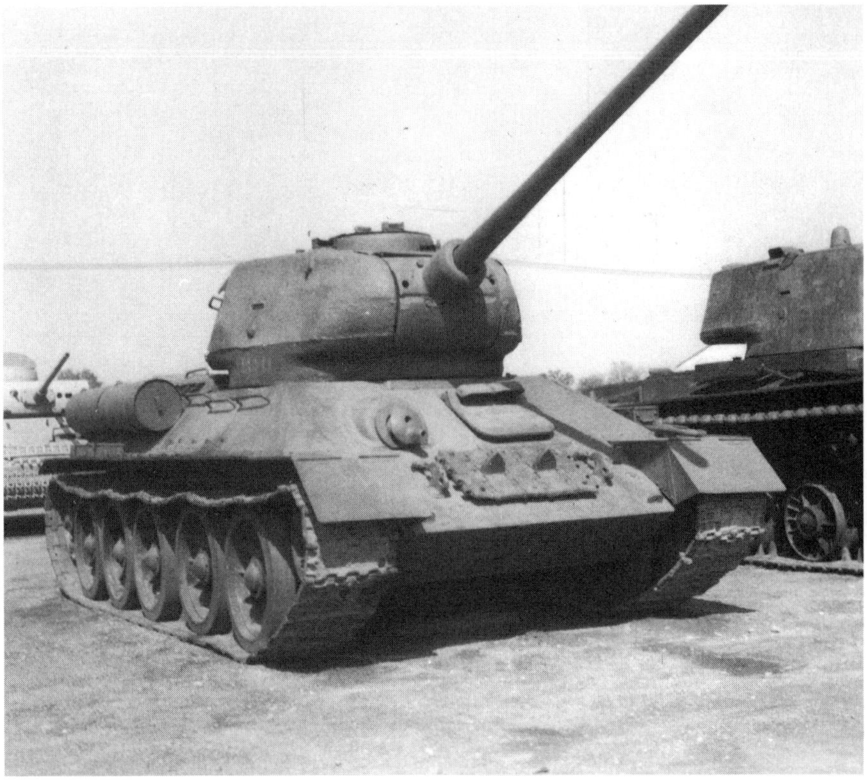

KV-13 prototype

1:35 scale

(76.2 mm ZIS-5 gun version)

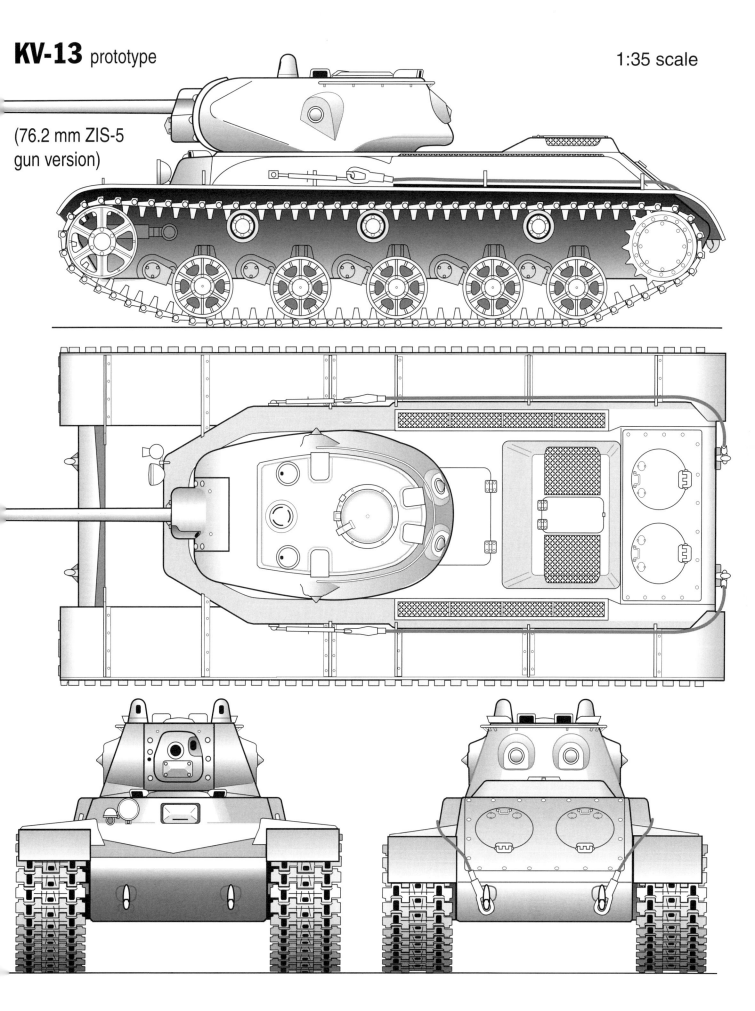

IS-3 Model 1945

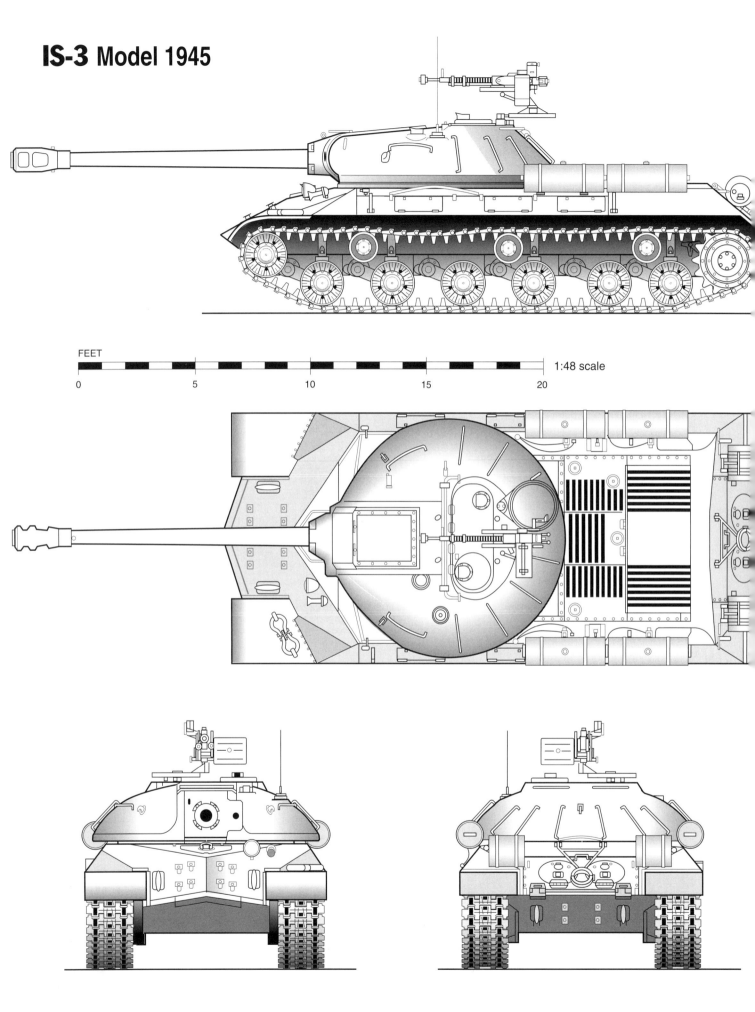

FEET

1:48 scale

0　　　　　5　　　　　10　　　　　15　　　　　20

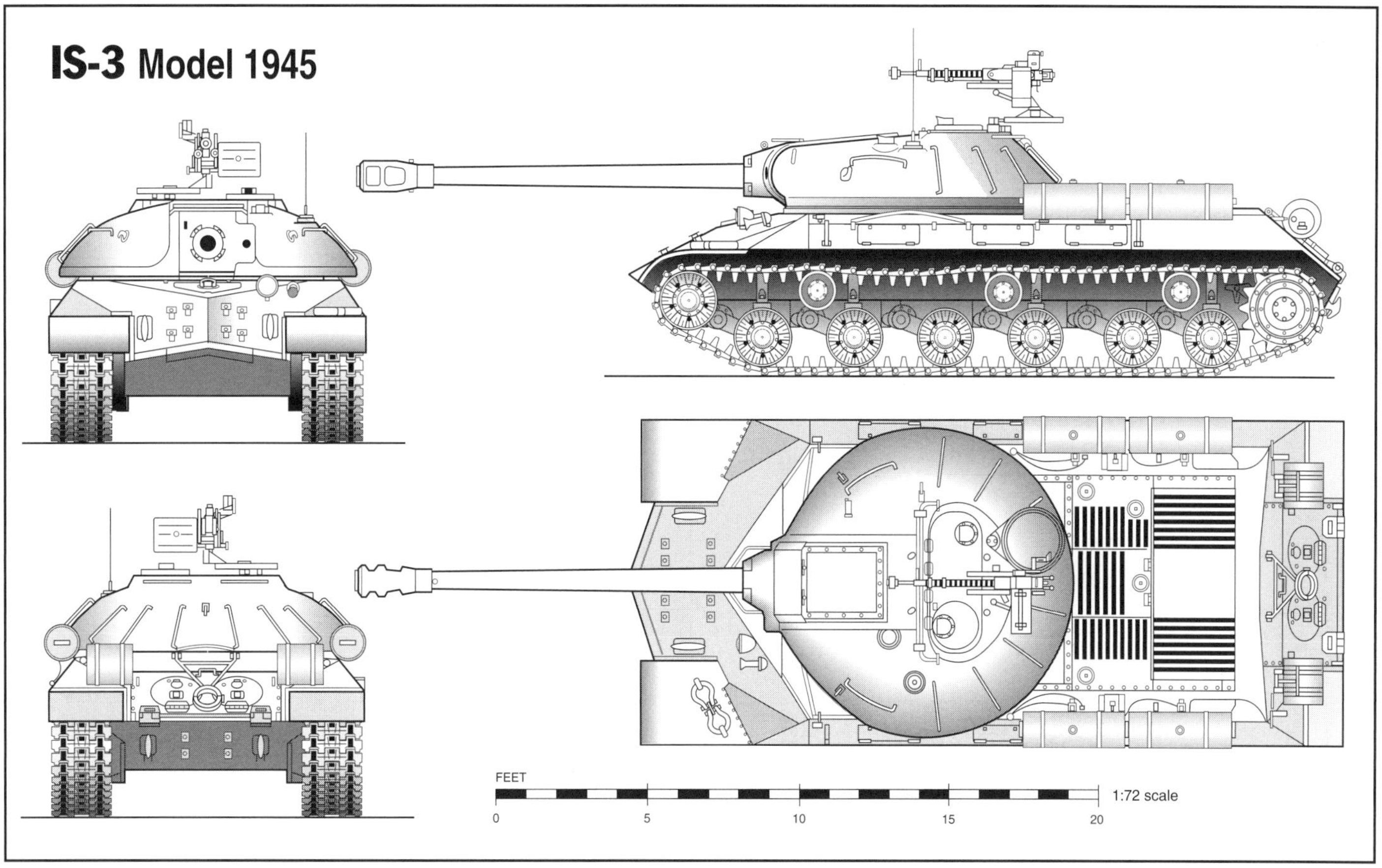
IS-3 Model 1945
FEET
0
5
10
15
20
1:72 scale

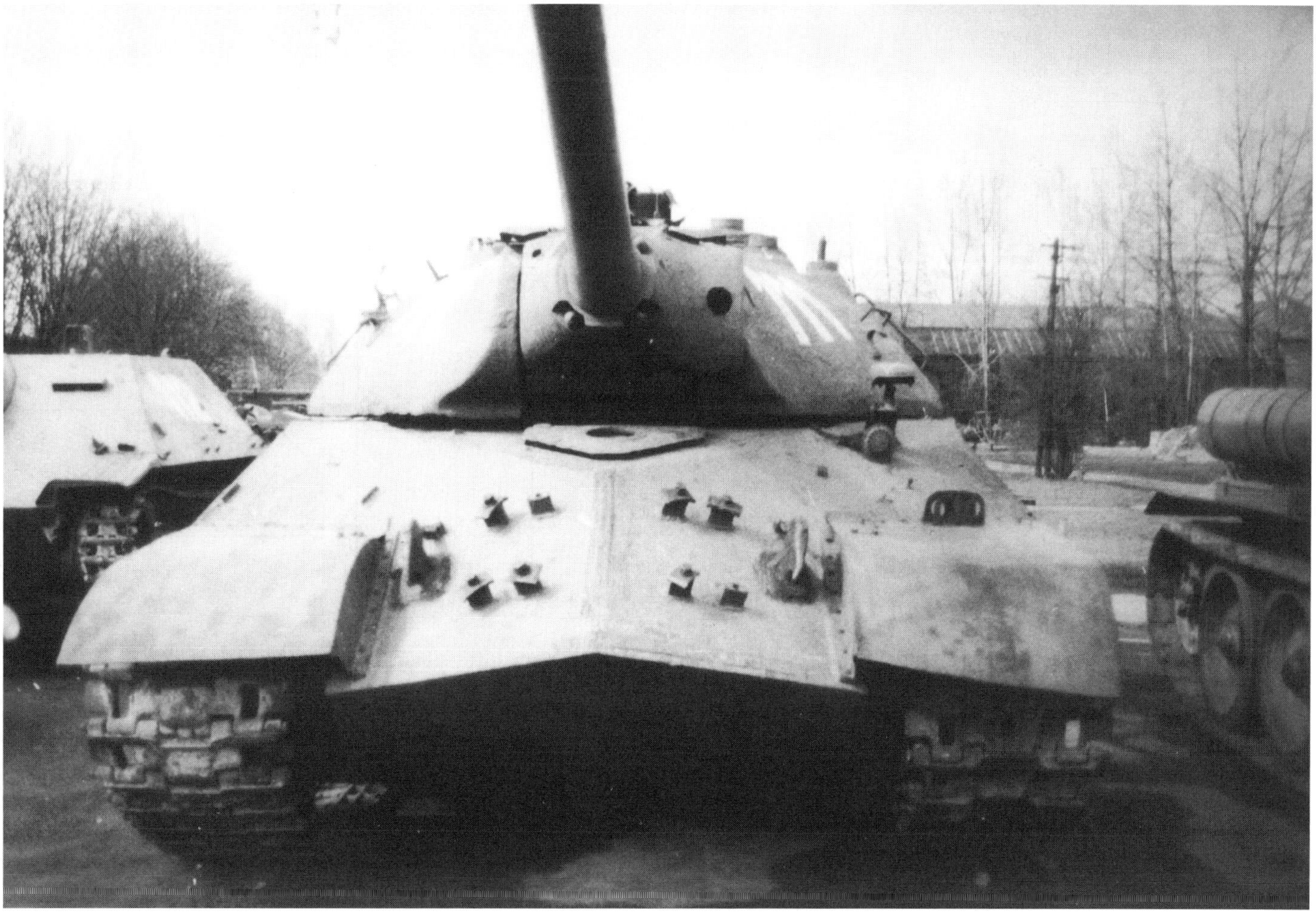

T-44 (Production Model)

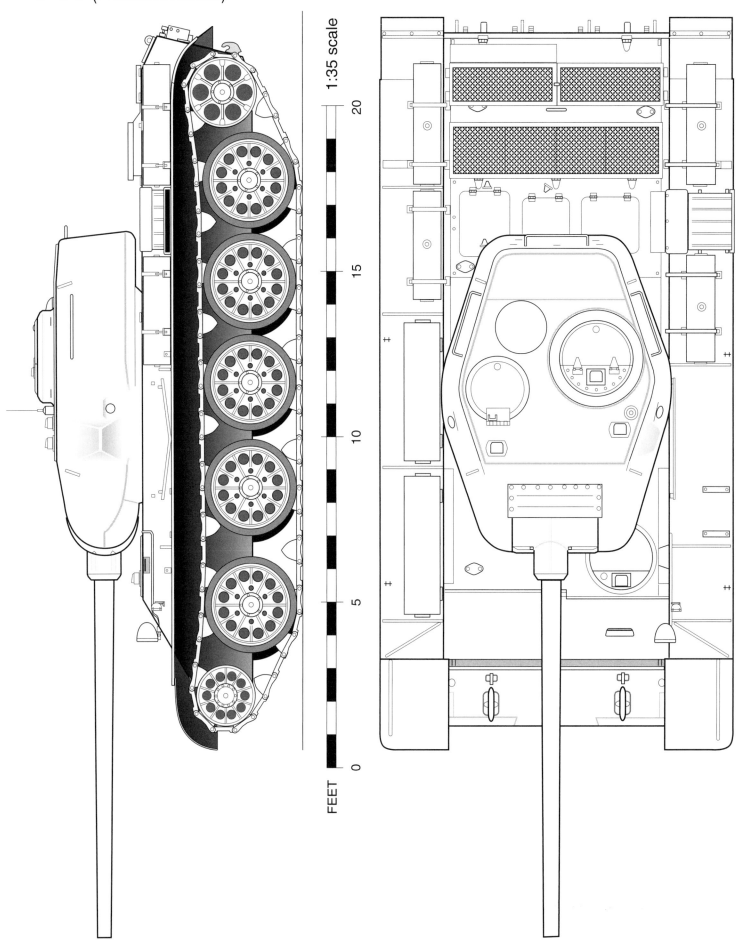

1:35 scale

FEET

0   5   10   15   20

T-44 (Production Model)

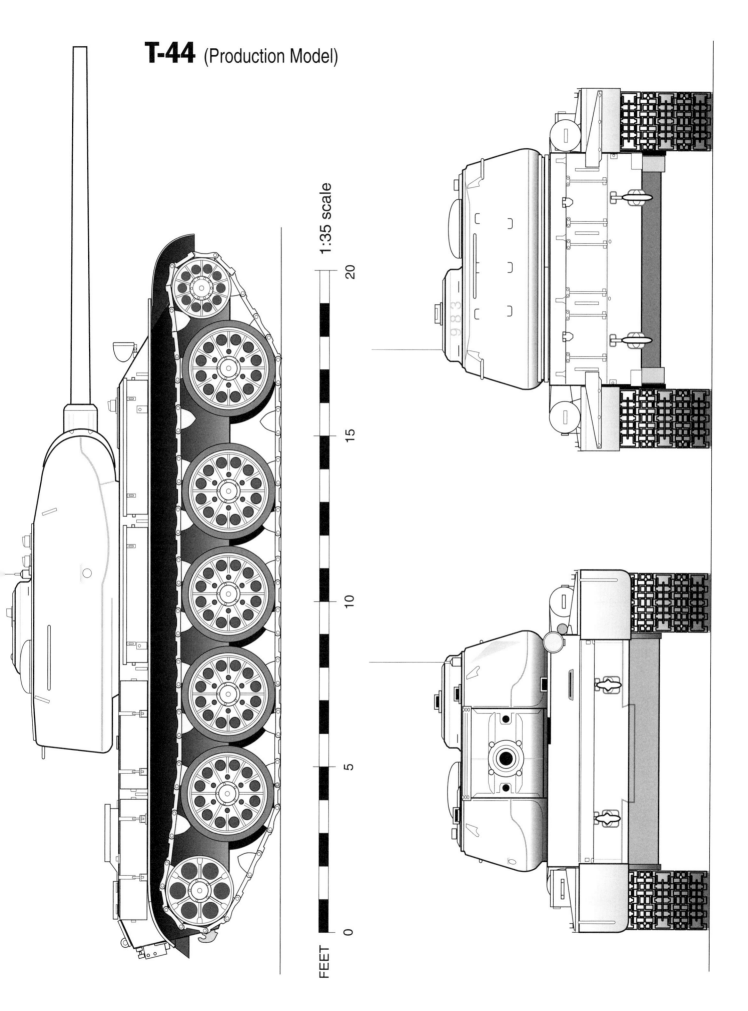

1:35 scale

20

15

10

5

0

FEET

SU-101 "Uralmash-1" Tank Destroyer

Developed late in the war this type would have replaced the SU-100 in 1945.

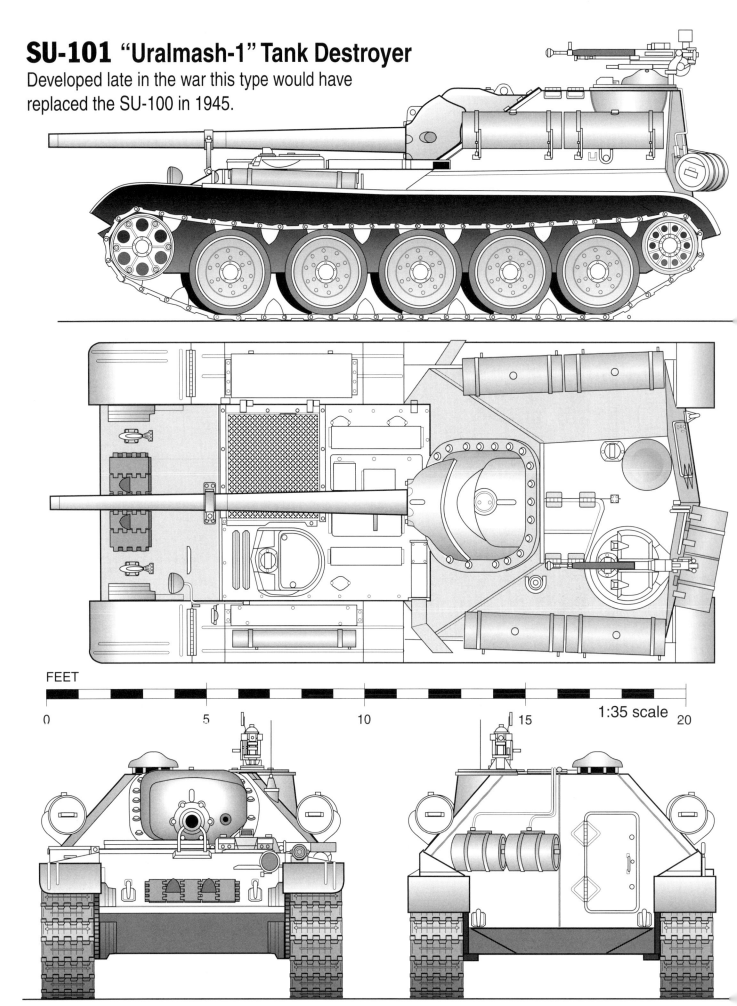

FEET

0   5   10   15   20

1:35 scale

IS-7 Heavy Tank (1948 prototype)

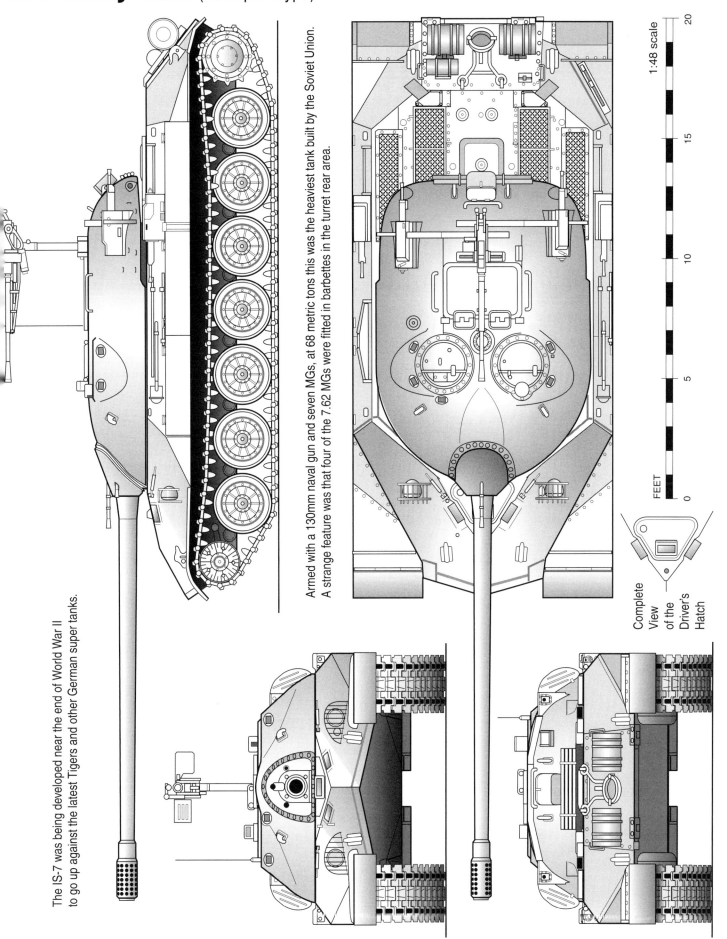

The IS-7 was being developed near the end of World War II to go up against the latest Tigers and other German super tanks.

Armed with a 130mm naval gun and seven MGs, at 68 metric tons this was the heaviest tank built by the Soviet Union. A strange feature was that four of the 7.62 MGs were fitted in barbettes in the turret rear area.

FEET

1:48 scale

0   5   10   15   20

Complete
View
of the
Driver's
Hatch

Bibliography

Chamberlain, P., and C. Ellis. *Tanks of the World, 1915–45*. London: Arms and Armour Press, 1972.

Crow, D., and R. J. Icks. *Encyclopedia of Armoured Cars*. Secaucus, NJ: Chartwell Books Inc., 1976.

———. *Encyclopedia of Tanks*. London: Barrie & Jenkins Limited, 1975.

Dupouy, A. *Les Dossiers Des Vehicules Sovietiques*. No. 14, *Les Engines Blindes a Roues, Tome I*. Grenoble, France: Alain Dupouy, 1999.

———. *Les Dossiers Des Vehicules Sovietiques*. No. 15, *Les Engines Blindes a Roues, Tome II*. Grenoble, France: Alain Dupouy, 1999.

Forty, G. *A Photo History of Armoured Cars in Two World Wars*. Poole, UK: Blandford Press, 1984.

Foss, C.F. *The Encyclopedia of Tanks and Armoured Fighting Vehicles*. London: Amber Books Ltd., 2002.

Halberstadt, H. *Inside the Great Tanks*. London: Windrow & Greene, 1997.

Icks, Robert J. *Tanks and Armored Vehicles, 1900–1945*. Old Greenwich, CT: We Inc., 1967.

Kolomyjec, M. *KW*. Vol. II, *1941–1944*. Warsaw, Poland: Wydawnictwo Militaria, 2002.

Magnuski, J. *Armor in Profile 1*. Warsaw, Poland: Pelta, 1997.

———. *Ciezki Czolg KW, Czolgi w Boju 4* Warsaw, Poland: Pelta, Warsaw, 1997.

———. *Czerwony Blitzkrieg*. Warsaw, Poland: Pelta, 1994.

———. *Wozy Bojowe*. Warsaw, Poland: Wydawnictwo Ministerswa Obrony Narodowej, 1964.

———. *Wozy Bojowe LWP 1943–1983*. Warsaw, Poland: Wydawnictwo Ministerswa Obrony Nar., 1985.

Regenberg, W. *Beutpanzer Unterm Balkenkreuz: Russische Kampfpanzer*. Friedberg, Germany: Podzun-Pallas-Verlag GmbH, 1989.

Skulski, P. *Seria "Pod Lupa" 101: T-34/76*. Wroclaw, Poland: Ace Publication, 1997.

Zaloga, S. J. and J. Magnuski. *IS-2 Heavy Tank, 1944–1973*. London: Osprey New Vanguard, 1996.

———. *Soviet Tanks and Combat Vehicles of World War Two*. London: Arms and Armour Press, 1984.

Basic Tank Components

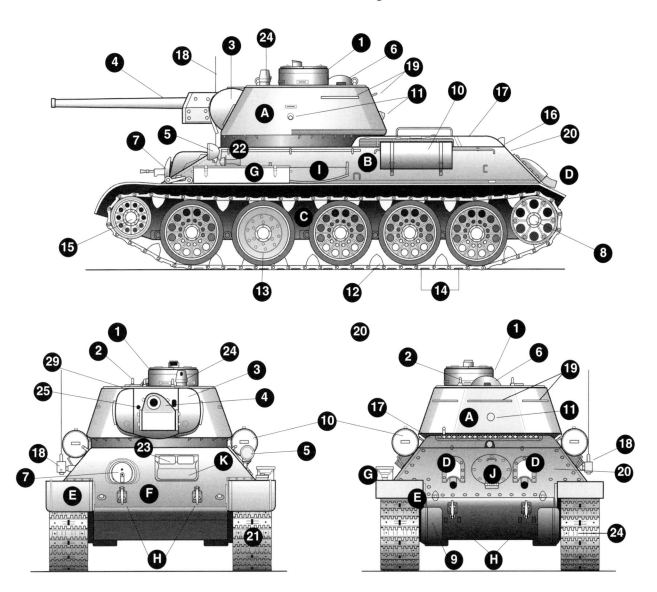

A. Cast Turret
B. Sloped Upper Hull
C. Lower Hull
D. Exhaust Pipes
E. Front Fender
F. Glacis Plate
G. Tool Box
H. Towing Brackets
I. Saw
J. Engine Access Door
K. Driver's Hatch

1. Commander's Cupola
2. Turret Lift Hook
3. Gun Mantlet
4. Main Gun
5. Headlamp
6. Ventilator
7. Bow Machinegun
8. Drive Sprocket
9. Transmission Housing
10. Spare Fuel Cannister
11. Pistol Port
12. Track Tooth
13. Road Wheel
14. Track Links

15. Front Idler Wheel
16. Tail Light
17. Engine Deck
18. Radio Aerial
19. Grab Rails
20. Rear Plate
21. Track Shoe
22. Siren
23. Driver's Visor
24. Periscope
25. Coaxial Machine Gun

VARIOUS MODELING SCALES

Scale	1 inch equals	1 scale foot =	1 scale meter =	Comments
1:4	4"	3"	250.0 mm	Flying Models, Live-steam Trains
1:8	8"	1 $^1/_2$"	125.0 mm	Cars, Motorcycles, Trains
1:12	1'	1"	83.3 mm	Cars, Motorcycles, Dollhouses
1:16	1' 4"	$^3/_4$"	62.5 mm	Cars, Motorcycles, Trains
1:20	1' 8"	$^{19}/_{32}$"	50.0 mm	Cars
1:22.5	1' 10$^1/_2$"	$^{17}/_{32}$"	44.4 mm	G-Scale Trains
1:24	2'	$^1/_2$"	41.7 mm	Cars, Trucks, Dollhouses
1:25	2' 1"	$^{15}/_{32}$"	40.0 mm	Cars, Trucks
1:32	2' 8"	$^3/_8$"	31.25 mm	Aircraft, Cars, Tanks, Trains
1:35	2' 11"	$^{11}/_{32}$"	28.57 mm	Armor
1:43	3' 7"	$^9/_{32}$"	23.25 mm	Cars, Trucks
1:48	4'	$^1/_4$"	20.83 mm	Aircraft, Armor, O-Scale Trains
1:64	5' 4"	$^3/_{16}$"	15.62 mm	Aircraft, S-Scale Trains
1:72	6'	$^{11}/_{63}$"	13.88 mm	Aircraft, Armor, Boats
1:76	6' 4"	$^5/_{32}$"	13.16 mm	Armor
1:87	7' 3"	—	11.49 mm	Armor, HO-Scale Trains
1:96	8'	$^1/_8$"	10.42 mm	$^1/_8$" Scale Ships, Aircraft
1:100	8' 4"	—	10.00 mm	Aircraft
1:125	10' 5"	—	8.00 mm	Aircraft
1:144	12'	—	6.94 mm	Aircraft
1:160	13' 4"	—	6.25 mm	N-Scale Trains
1:192	16'	$^1/_{16}$"	5.21 mm	$^1/_{16}$" Scale Ships
1:200	16' 8"	—	5.00 mm	Aircraft, Ships

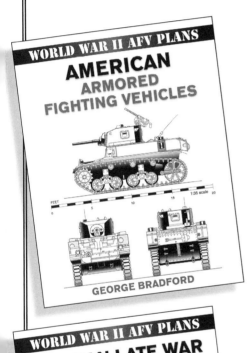

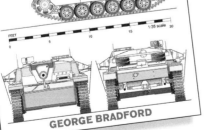